The Sisters of
Battle Road

J. M. MALONEY
The Sisters of Battle Road

The extraordinary true story of six
sisters evacuated from wartime London

CORGI BOOKS

TRANSWORLD PUBLISHERS
61–63 Uxbridge Road, London W5 5SA
www.penguin.co.uk

Transworld is part of the Penguin Random House group of companies
whose addresses can be found at global.penguinrandomhouse.com

First published in Great Britain in 2017 by Corgi Books
an imprint of Transworld Publishers

This book is a work of non-fiction based on the life, experiences and
recollections of the author's family. The author has stated to the publishers
that the contents of this book are true.

A CIP catalogue record for this book
is available from the British Library.

ISBN 9780552174077

Typeset in 11/13.5 pt Berkeley by Jouve (UK), Milton Keynes
Printed and bound in Great Britain by Clays Ltd, Bungay, Suffolk

Penguin Random House is committed to a sustainable
future for our business, our readers and our planet. This book
is made from Forest Stewardship Council® certified paper.

1 3 5 7 9 10 8 6 4 2

This book can only really be dedicated to Mary, Joan, Sheila, Kath, Pat and Anne, whose story it is. But it is also for the grandparents I never knew, Pierce and Annie. Through their daughters I enjoyed discovering something about their lives. I feel a little closer to them now.

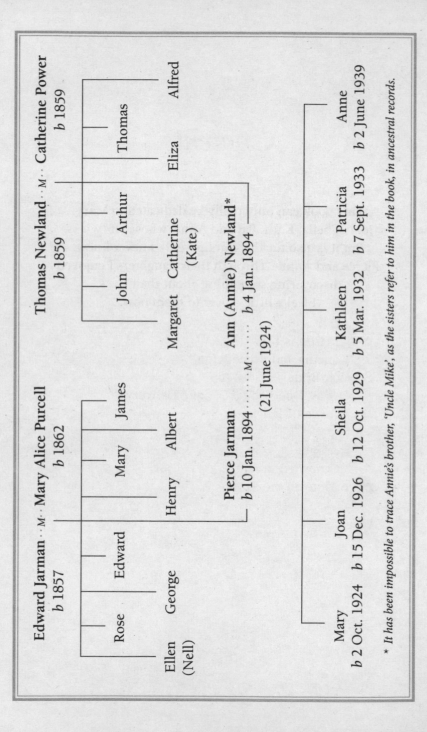

Edward Jarman ·· M ·· Mary Alice Purcell
b 1857   b 1862

Ellen   George   Edward   Henry   Mary   Albert   James
(Nell)   Rose

Pierce Jarman ······ M ······· Ann (Annie) Newland*
b 10 Jan. 1894   b 4 Jan. 1894
              (21 June 1924)

Thomas Newland ·· M ·· Catherine Power
b 1859   b 1859

Margaret   John   Arthur   Catherine   Eliza   Thomas   Alfred
                           (Kate)

Mary   Joan   Sheila   Kathleen   Patricia   Anne
b 2 Oct. 1924 b 15 Dec. 1926 b 12 Oct. 1929 b 5 Mar. 1932 b 7 Sept. 1933 b 2 June 1939

* It has been impossible to trace Annie's brother, 'Uncle Mike', as the sisters refer to him in the book, in ancestral records.

Contents

Prologue   1

1   All or None   5
2   Battle Road   31
3   Fitting In   59
4   The Telegram   99
5   All for One   127
6   Christmas Tear   159
7   Dancing and Romancing   191
8   War Bride   223
9   D-Day, Doodlebugs . . . and Delivery   245
10 Farewell, Hailsham   271

    Epilogue   285
    Acknowledgements   289
    A Note on the Author   290

Prologue

Annie.

'Sheila!'

A weak voice called out from one of the bedrooms at 18 Battle Road. Hearing the call, a girl ran towards it quickly. Squinting through the dim light in the sparsely furnished room, she could see her mother, Annie, lying on the bed.

'Will you wash my hair for me, love, if you have time?' Annie asked quietly. 'I'd like to look half decent.'

At eleven years old, Sheila was always happy to do anything she could to help her mother, and during this latest bout of crippling illness, which had seen Annie in and out of hospital and confined to bed for weeks, she was more eager than ever.

Rushing back to the kitchen at the other end of the hallway, she boiled a pan of water on the stove, then poured it into a large tin jug. Carefully carrying it back to the bedroom, she set it down on the little wooden table next to Annie's bed, before returning to the kitchen to grab two bowls from the cupboard, a spoon from the drawer and a packet of Oxydol soap powder from under the sink.

Wartime rationing and shortage of money meant they could no longer obtain the jar of soft soap that they once used to wash their hair. Now they had to look for alternative options. Sheila picked up the soap powder, which they used to clean their clothes, and shook some of it into the smaller of the two bowls. Adding a little water, she stirred it to form a paste.

Gently helping to ease her mother up into a sitting position, she put a loving arm behind Annie's narrow shoulders and adjusted the crumpled pillows. Standing at her side, she poured the warm water over Annie's bent head, using the second bowl to catch the drops beneath. Then, she gently massaged the soap paste into her mother's hair before rinsing it out. With a towel, she dried her thinning hair and combed it through tenderly.

'Thanks, love,' said Annie.

Sheila looked at her mother with concern. 'You will still be here when I come home from school, won't you, Mummy?' she asked.

Annie smiled. 'Of course. You'll be home before I go.'

That evening, the ambulance arrived as planned. With a sinking heart but a determined smile, a frail Annie said goodbye to her five youngest children as the ambulance men carried her out to their vehicle, destined for a hospital ward in faraway London. The eldest daughter, Mary, had not yet returned home from work. Joan, the next oldest, was in charge. She picked up their two-year-old sister, Anne, and, cradling her in her arms, traipsed back up the stairs, followed by her three younger sisters. Spotting them at the upstairs window, Annie raised her thin, pale arm to wave goodbye and each girl waved back sadly, their eyes brimming with tears.

It was May 1941, the second year of country living for the six Jarman sisters, who had been evacuated from Bermondsey in South London to Hailsham in Sussex at the start of the Second World War. And everything was about to change.

Chapter 1
All or None

*The sisters of Abbey Street (from left to right)
Mary, Joan, Sheila and Kath.*

'WE'RE STAYING TOGETHER, whatever happens,' Annie Jarman told her six daughters. 'I won't let anyone split us up.'

It had been a long and tiring day for the Jarman family. Just the day before, German troops had crossed the border into Poland, and any hope of avoiding war now seemed lost. Having invaded Austria and Czechoslovakia, and announced plans to increase his military and naval strength massively, Hitler's influence and aggression as head of the Nazi party had continued to increase. The British Government had been discussing plans to move children from the cities and into safer parts of the countryside for years, should Germany start to bomb Britain, and now they were finally putting their grand evacuation scheme into place. And so it was that the Jarman sisters – Mary, fourteen; Joan, twelve; Sheila, nine; Kath, seven; Pat, five; and baby Anne – found themselves on a train with their mother, bound for Sussex, leaving behind the threat of the bombers but leaving their father too.

As she had a child under the age of five, Annie was one of the few mothers allowed to be evacuated with her offspring. This gave her great comfort – she couldn't imagine how less fortunate women were feeling – but at the same time she fretted that they might be split up when they reached their destination. They were, after all, a large family. Who would have space to take them all? Surely there was a limit to how kind and generous people could be? Her husband, Pierce, who tended to fret about his daughters' wellbeing at the best of times, had been equally worried.

'I don't want them separated. You've got to stay with them, Annie,' he'd said. 'Promise me.'

'Don't worry. I'm not letting them out of my sight,' she'd replied defiantly. 'It's all of us, or we come straight back home.' It was typical fighting talk, but neither Annie nor Pierce could fully appreciate just how difficult things were going to be.

On the morning of the evacuation, the Jarman household in Bermondsey's Abbey Street – always a lively place – had been a hive of activity. Pierce had said his goodbyes early, hugging and kissing each of his daughters in turn in the hallway, before leaving for work as a meter collector at the London Electricity Board.

'Be sure to help Mummy out as much as possible, won't you, Mary?' he'd said. 'You, too, Joan,' he added, turning towards his second oldest daughter. 'And keep an eye on the younger ones.'

Both girls smiled warmly at their father, assuring him that they would do as he asked. They were well used to chipping in with childcare and other domestic chores. They knew how much their mother depended on them, and they didn't want to let their father down.

Pierce, a tall, lean and pale-skinned man, took a deep breath, fighting back a swell of emotion. He smiled down at Sheila, looking pretty in her ringlets, as usual. While her sisters were excited about swapping London and their school for an adventure in the countryside, Sheila was adamant that she didn't want to leave her home and friends in Bermondsey.

'Don't look so glum, Sheila,' said Pierce reassuringly. 'You'll like the countryside. Plenty of quiet for you to enjoy your reading.'

Sheila did her best to muster a little smile. 'I want you to come with us,' she said in a small voice. She would miss everyone but the prospect of being without her father almost broke her heart.

'I know,' he replied. 'And I want to be with you too, but I have to work. And I'll be down every weekend.'

Kath jiggled her way to the front as Sheila took a step back. 'Will you be down this weekend, Dad?' she asked.

'Yes, of course,' he replied. 'As soon as I know where you are.' He paused. 'Be a good girl, won't you, Kath?' Pierce was only too aware that Kath, the most tomboyish of his daughters, had a particular tendency to scuffle with other girls, and her stubborn nature was legendary within the family. 'You too, Pat,' he added, looking over to a smaller clone of Kath with the same full-fringed bob hairstyle, standing just behind her sister.

Finally, Annie, holding baby Anne, stepped forward and Pierce kissed them both. 'Take care,' he said.

'Bye, darling.' Annie smiled. 'Love you. I'll write as soon as I can and let you know where we are.'

They shared one final kiss, then, after taking his cap out of his pocket and fixing it firmly on his head, Pierce opened the front door. His family spilled out behind him as he walked onto the grey London street with a heavy heart. How odd it would feel coming home that evening. Instead of hearing their familiar chatter, his wife and daughters would all be gone. Quite where to, he did not know. Like all evacuees and their families, no one was really sure where they were going and the anxiety was palpable. He'd never been without them before and although the idea of evacuation was to make them safer, he felt keenly that he wouldn't be in a position to protect them from danger. He'd never felt so helpless in his life.

At the end of the street, he turned and gave a final wave to his loved ones milling on the pavement outside the front door. Then he rounded the corner and felt more alone than ever before.

Living in a house full of females was not always easy for Pierce, who needed to escape some evenings, money permitting, to the sanctuary of the local pub for a pint and perhaps a game of darts or shove ha'penny – a simple pastime played on a wooden board in which coins would be knocked forward to score points. Nevertheless, he was still very much a family man and always looked forward to returning home after a long day at work emptying coin meters that supplied electricity in Bermondsey. But now he wondered how he would cope.

Pierce quickened his pace as he walked past grey-brick houses, determined not to keep thinking so negatively and nodding at various familiar men in flat caps also making their way to work. Besides, he wouldn't be on his own entirely. The family shared the house with Annie's parents, who had the ground floor, and his three sisters lived just a few streets away. They had always been very protective of their brother and reassured him that they would look after him now, cook for him and do his washing, and he could stay with them whenever he wanted.

Pierce might have been feeling melancholy on his journey to work but back at the house there was simply no time for such thoughts. After her husband had left, Annie put her mind once more to the job of organizing six children. Their belongings had to be packed into bags and there was a crying baby to settle. The stress and heightened emotion were taking their toll but there was no time to waste. Although she had laid out clothes the night before, last-minute additions, such as soap and toothbrushes, needed to be added.

They'd been told that each child could take a suitcase but Annie and Pierce didn't have the money to buy such items for their girls. So, like many other evacuees with limited means, the Jarmans improvised: they packed up their belongings in school satchels, carrier bags and brown paper packages tied up with string. They looked like a ragtag mob, thought Annie, but needs must. Most people were in the same boat.

The Government had provided guidelines of what to pack and Annie kept referring to the leaflet, checking and double-checking that she had not forgotten anything. They hoped they wouldn't be gone long – no one could believe a war was really coming – but there was always a chance that they wouldn't see home again for a long time. For girls, the list included dresses, blouses, underwear, cardigans and handkerchiefs, along with toiletries and something to eat on the journey, such as a sandwich, an apple and some biscuits, and a drink. It was vitally important not to forget the gas masks – which could hang around the girls' necks – and their identity cards, which Annie pinned carefully to their coats. There would be a lot of people travelling; it would be a disaster to get lost.

Four schools from Bermondsey were set to travel together, assembling at Pages Walk School before walking the ten minutes to London Bridge station where they would board a train to take them away to the countryside. Now, with time seeming to fly and despite her careful planning, Annie was panicking that they would never be ready in time and would miss the train.

'Girls! Keep the noise down!' she shouted as she tried to cram a final few favourite possessions – a framed family photograph and her perfume bottle – into her battered old brown case.

'Mum, have you seen my flannel?'

Annie, her temper rising, turned to Kath. 'Have you washed this morning?' she asked.

Kath nodded.

'Well, for goodness' sake, Kath, it will be where you left it.'

'I can't see it,' said Kath.

'Well, have another look!'

As Kath walked off, Annie called after her, 'And make sure your hands are scrubbed extra clean! Nobody's going to take in dirty children.'

Of all her daughters, Kath was the one most likely to come home with grubby hands, grazed knees and dishevelled hair, and her younger sister, Pat, was showing signs of following in her footsteps. Annie had often marvelled at how different her daughters were. In stark contrast to Kath and Pat, Sheila was much more feminine in nature and looked forward to having her hair put into trailing ringlets by her mother every morning before she left for school. And while Joan was practical and sensible, Mary had a more carefree nature, which made her quite accident-prone. Two years previously, in the school Christmas production of *Snow White and the Seven Dwarves*, she had fallen off the stage whilst dressed as Dopey – she had wanted to be Snow White – and Annie hadn't forgotten the sight of her clambering back up onto the stage, her wire ears all bent out of shape, whilst the audience howled with laughter.

So when Annie – in the process of sitting on her bulging suitcase and doing up the clasps – heard a tumbling noise on the stairs, she knew instinctively who it was. Rushing out of her bedroom, she saw Mary on her backside at the bottom of the staircase.

'I slipped,' said Mary, slowly getting to her feet. 'I didn't want to miss the train.'

'If you break your neck, then we won't be able to go at all,' her mother retorted.

Somehow they all managed to get their bags packed and make it to the front door, where everyone waited while Annie did a last-minute check that they had everything they needed. Annie's parents, Tom and Catherine (known to her friends as Kate), stood in their customary formal fashion as each child took their turn to give them a peck on the cheek and a rather awkward little hug. Annie gave them both a kiss and an embrace herself, and felt a lump in her throat.

'You take care,' said Kate, who, like her husband, felt it was not the thing to show too much emotion. With that, Annie and her girls trundled outside and set off on foot to Pages Walk School, off the Old Kent Road, and the beginning of a new life.

In the school playground, as more and more families arrived, the noise became almost unbearably loud. Anxious mums shared their concerns with each other and excitable children chatted and played. Teachers, local authority officials and volunteer marshals attempted to keep order whilst names were checked off the list. It was no easy task in the tumult, but somehow they managed it.

A long centipede of children and attendant adults eventually began to snake its way through the streets of Bermondsey, along to Grange Road, before crossing Tower Bridge Road, where they could see the famous old bridge looming in the distance. Intermittent calls from the adult supervisors of 'Keep together!' and 'Hurry along!' were heard along the way as the procession then headed up Bermondsey Street to London Bridge station. Some of the youngsters were smiling and laughing as if off on a summer holiday – there were certainly plenty who had never left London before – while others were in a quieter, more sombre mood, aware that this extraordinary event was a very serious matter.

Emotions ran even higher once the children started to board the waiting train and gave their tearful parents one last farewell hug, neither knowing what the future held. Many mothers, unable to contain themselves, wept openly and some of the children broke down, too. The Jarman girls chatted excitedly, though – they were, after all, amongst the lucky ones who didn't have to face the trauma of having to leave their mother behind.

In the weeks leading up to evacuation, government posters had been plastered all over London proclaiming the likes of 'Children are safer in the country. Leave them there' and 'Mothers. Send them out of London. Give them a chance of greater safety and health'. Nevertheless, with their children's tear-stained faces pressed to the windows as the train started to chug away from the platform, some parents doubted whether they had made the right decision.

As the train made its way out of London into a greener

environment, the babble of chatter increased. The acres of fields were an eye-opener for many who had never been away from home before, and the sight of cows, sheep and horses caused much pointing, gasping and giggling. With a few countryside trips under their belt, the Jarman sisters felt much more worldly wise, even if the trips had mostly been for recuperation purposes.

The health benefits of clean, rural air, in contrast to the smoggy pollution of London, had long been advocated by health officials. When she was younger, Mary had contracted a bad case of bronchitis every year and, at the age of seven, had been sent to a charitable convalescent home in Dover, run by Catholic nuns. There, she and other children would attend mass every day, and sleep in long dormitories at night and outside on camp beds in the fresh air during fine days.

She had hated it there. The journey to Dover was too far and too expensive for her parents and sisters to visit her much, so she had often felt lonely. However, her convalescence did leave her with one lovely memory. It had been a Sunday afternoon and, while she was sleeping, a nun came in and woke her by gently placing a baby on her bed. A sleepy Mary looked down to see that it was her sister, Kath, then only a few months old. Mary was delighted to see her again and knew that it meant that her parents were there also. As she sat up and looked across the room, she saw them smiling at her from the doorway.

During her two months in Dover, Mary was fed so well that when she returned home she had put on so much weight that most of her clothes were too small for her! As she sat on the train now, in the back of her mind she was hoping against hope for something good to come of this latest upheaval.

Another year, before little Anne was born, the charitable Bermondsey Medical Mission in Grange Road, which provided medical care for women and children in the area, had sent the five Jarman sisters to the seaside town of Ramsgate on the south coast when they all caught whooping cough. Annie had gone with them too and they had stayed with a kindly lady who provided them with nourishing food and, if they were spending the day on the beach, a picnic of sandwiches, cakes and drinks, much to their delight.

They loved playing on the beach, feeling the sand between their toes and the tickle of cold seawater licking at their ankles. They soon found out that their pale, urban complexions were unsuitable for long periods in the sun, however, when two-year-old Pat, to her painful cost, sunburnt her arms. They'd all been excited by their countryside stay, though, and now, even for the nervous Sheila, there was a sense that they were once again on the cusp of a huge adventure.

As the train full of evacuees made its way southwards, Pat was called over to the window by Kath.

'Look, Pat,' said her older sister, taking on the air of a teacher instructing a pupil. 'Cows.'

Pat joined Kath at the window, which was framed with rust-coloured grime, and Joan also took a look. They stared out over unfamiliar fields.

'It's too warm today but if they lie down, that means it's going to rain,' said Joan with some authority.

'How would they know it's going to rain?' asked a puzzled Kath. 'That can't be true.'

Annie, sitting beside the girls with a sleeping Anne on her lap, smiled at the familiar banter between the girls. They could always find something to disagree about.

All or None

The train stopped eventually at Polegate in Sussex, where the evacuees clambered out like gaggling geese from the back of a truck.

'Move away from the track!' shouted a guard over the sound of train doors slamming.

The children looked around quickly, wondering what was coming next. As they were ushered on to the station forecourt, they discovered that this was not the end of their journey. Several coaches were parked there in a line, their drivers chatting together and smoking cigarettes as they stared over at the army of children approaching them.

The teachers met up with the local volunteers and, after a short discussion, names were called out from a list and told to get on to the first coach. The Jarman family stood and observed, waiting to be called. One by one the coaches pulled away, leaving just one. Finally, the Jarmans heard their names announced and they boarded the remaining coach with several other evacuees but, the girls noticed, only a few of their school friends, including the seven Eddicott children and their mother, Mary, who was also a friend of Annie's. Amidst the strangeness of it all, they were thankful to be with the Eddicotts and the many children huddled together on board the coach.

'Have something to eat, girls,' said Annie, once they were on their way. 'But make sure you save some for later,' she added, not knowing when their next meal would be.

The coach made its way along quiet, pretty country roads, the children silent now, intrigued to reach their final destination. It was all so very different from London, thought Annie, and then, not for the first time that day, her mind turned to Pierce. What might he be doing right now? And how would he feel when he returned home after work? But then she smiled to herself. He'll probably be off down the pub!

It was a short coach ride and, after alighting, the girls looked for their other friends but could only see volunteers with armbands, acting as billeting officers, who led them into a stuffy community hall in Summerheath Road, Hailsham.

Annie caught up with Miss Mobbs, a teacher from a school in Rotherhithe, which neighboured Bermondsey. 'Where's everyone else? The other coachloads?' she asked.

'They've gone to Lewes,' Miss Mobbs replied. 'This is Hailsham.'

Annie hadn't considered that the community might be separated. The prospect of being amongst strangers worried her and she felt a churning of anxiety in her tummy.

Inside the hall a variety of people – individual children, siblings and those with mothers – stood in clusters as soft drinks, tea and biscuits were passed around. A steady procession of local homeowners arrived throughout the day, scrutinizing what looked to them like pale, shabby and rather undernourished Londoners. 'Hosts' were paid an allowance of 10s 6d per week if they took one child into their home and 8s 6d per week for each extra child. Pretty girls and strong, healthy boys were picked first while grubbier and more sickly looking children were further down the pecking order. Annie spotted how it worked straight away.

'It's just like a cattle market in here,' she muttered to Mary Eddicott. Like Annie, Mary too was determined to keep her children together, and both women knew that would be a challenge.

'I could maybe take these two,' said one middle-aged woman to a billeting officer, as she eyed up Mary and Joan. 'If they can muck in on the farm,' she added.

The officer looked at Annie expectantly.

'We'll all be staying together,' said Annie determinedly.

'I can't take all of you,' said the woman, raising her eyebrows in surprise.

'We're a family. We can't be split up,' insisted Annie.

As the day wore on, it remained a similar story. If the girls didn't like the look of anyone, they would try to hide behind each other, desperate not to make eye contact. When the skies began to darken, and fewer and fewer children were left in the hall, it became evident that nobody wanted to take in such a large family, especially not one with the mother in tow.

What had started out as an exciting adventure for the girls had become decidedly less so as they became increasingly tired, hungry and irritable. 'How much longer, Mum?' they complained. 'I'm sleepy.'

Towards the end of the afternoon there were just three large families left in the hall – the Jarmans, the Eddicotts and their other friends from Bermondsey, Hannah Philpott and her seven children.

If Annie was maintaining a bold front, Mary, usually the most optimistic and the biggest giggler of the sisters, was starting to worry.

'What if no one wants us, Mum?' she said. 'Maybe we will have to split up.'

Annie, true to her nature, remained firm. 'I said we're staying together and I meant it,' she replied.

The Sisters of Battle Road

Back home in Bermondsey, Mary had always rued the fact that she – like her sisters and their father – had bright-red hair. Not because of any notion of vanity but because it made her stand out and was instantly recognizable when being naughty – usually nothing much more than giggling or talking in class. Now, ironically, when Mary and her sisters needed to catch people's attention the most, they were being ignored.

The afternoon had started with the girls – under their mother's strict instructions – doing their best to look presentable, smile and not fidget, but the younger sisters, Kath and Pat, were becoming restless and hungry, and just wanted to go back home. It wasn't fun any more. Their anxiety increased further when the Philpotts were led away to be given accommodation in vacant rooms over an empty shop. That left just two families.

With no takers, the Jarmans and Eddicotts were led to the church hall next to the grand red-brick, three-storey, seventeenth-century vicarage, which had a pretty garden and a sweeping drive. Inside the hall, fifteen camp beds had been set out along the walls.

'It looks like a hospital!' Annie joked. It wasn't ideal but she was grateful to have somewhere, anywhere, for the family to sleep that night, whatever the following morning might bring.

'Is this where we'll be staying?' asked Kath in wide-eyed wonderment.

'It's just temporary, Kath. Until they find us somewhere else,' Joan assured her. 'A proper home,' she added, although she was beginning to have her doubts.

They were supplied with tins of corned beef, potatoes, rice, hot chocolate and some rather hard biscuits. The nourishment was most welcome and, despite so many children in such a confined space, it was easy to get comfortable and relax – after such a long day they were all exhausted. There was little chatter that evening as they got ready for bed but there were plenty of yawns, and it wasn't long before everyone fell asleep.

Back in Bermondsey, Pierce had just returned home from the pub and was in the kitchen making a cup of tea. He picked up the government leaflet about evacuation, entitled 'Why and How'. Perusing the pages, he slowed down at a section sub-headed 'Work Must Go On'. It read, 'For most of us who do not go off to the Fighting Forces, our duty will be to stand by our jobs.' It went on, 'There can be no question of wholesale clearance' because 'We are not going to win a war by running away.'

Standing alone in the silent kitchen, he wondered where Annie and his daughters had run away to and whether they would ever come back.

Annie and the girls awoke to another hot and sunny day. Outside, the children thought how different everything looked here. The trees, country roads and paths, and the fields in the distance were in sharp contrast to the grey houses and maze of streets of Bermondsey. It was so quiet too. Dockhead was a hive of activity and noise. Running along the Thames, incorporating London Bridge and Tower Bridge, it had thriving factories and food markets as a consequence of the passage of ships importing and exporting goods up the river.

The girls spent the day playing in the grounds around the church hall in Hailsham, and also walked through the cemetery of the picture-postcard St Mary's Church, a charming structure built of stone with a red-tiled roof and a tower to one end, dating back to the early fifteenth century. While the children amused themselves, the mothers sat in the sunshine, discussing what the future might hold for them. War seemed a million miles away from this tranquil and pretty little corner of England.

'Hard to believe it's even going to happen when you're sitting here, all peaceful,' said Annie.

'I was just thinking the same,' said Mary Eddicott. 'Maybe it'll all come to nothing and we can go home.'

Annie glanced towards Kath and Pat, who were lying on the grass, playing with a delighted Anne. 'I hope so,' she whispered. 'For their sake.'

The two mothers felt increasingly anxious about their fate as the day wore on. Despite regular visits from local volunteers, who shared kind words along with food and drink, it was to be another night on their camp beds, still wondering where they would end up.

The following morning was a Sunday and Annie made sure that her girls were up and ready for mass at the little Catholic church, St Wilfrid's, on South Road. Neither Annie or Pierce went to church themselves, but they insisted that their daughters attended on a regular basis. The girls were only too aware that if they skipped mass they would face interrogation from the nuns at school, who would ask probingly exactly what the priest had talked about in his sermon that particular week.

St Wilfrid's was only a short distance from the church hall and the girls enjoyed exploring some of the village en route. As they walked along country roads dotted with houses of various architectural styles, including red-brick farm dwellings, mock Tudor houses, and more contemporary detached and semi-detached homes with bay windows, the girls were amazed at how much space there was in the countryside.

The red-brick Catholic church was small and unimposing, just one room with wooden pews, seating fewer than fifty people, and a simple altar. Nevertheless, the girls were nervous, so they were pleased – and relieved – to see that the Philpotts had arrived before them. Hannah Philpott was a very religious woman and not one to miss mass just because she had been uprooted from her home and a world war was looming. Indeed, it was all the more reason to go.

The evacuees' presence at church attracted some attention from the local parishioners and the priest welcomed them warmly.

'I notice some new faces here this morning,' he said with a smile. 'How lovely to see you. Welcome. And I hope to see more of you and get to know you all in the coming weeks.'

The girls thought this service much more informal than the ones they were used to back home in the large, imposing, gothic-style Most Holy Trinity Church in Dockhead. They never knew churches like St Wilfrid's existed and found themselves enjoying the experience, almost able to imagine themselves as part of this new community.

Service over, they were making their way back to the vicarage when, at eleven o'clock, an air-raid siren sounded. Frightened, and imagining that they would be gas-bombed at any moment – as leaflets and posters back in Bermondsey had warned – they ran as fast as they could back to the church hall. They had seen many demonstrations on how to fit their gas masks, but it was the first time they had had to use them, and they found themselves all fingers and thumbs.

'Come on,' Annie said, calming the girls down. 'You remember what to do, don't you?'

Annie had baby Anne to think about. Parents with children under the age of two were issued with a scary-looking contraption, comprising a steel helmet with a visor for the baby to see through, and Annie had been horrified when first instructed how to use it. The attached canvas section, rubber-coated on the inside, was folded under the baby and fastened underneath with straps while the infant's legs dangled freely. An asbestos filter on the side of the mask was meant to absorb any poisonous gases that might seep in, and attached to this was a rubber, concertinaed tube which was pumped to provide oxygen.

Annie hated the thought of enclosing her baby in this machine, relying on the pump mechanism to keep her alive, but she knew that it was designed to save lives. So she put Anne in it, as gently as she could, whispering in her daughter's ear in soothing and reassuring tones to keep her calm.

Then, looking at her two eldest children, her face took on a sombre expression. 'If anything should happen to me,' she began, faltering for a moment, before continuing, 'you must make sure to keep pumping air into the baby's gas mask. You know how to do it, don't you?'

Mary and Joan were too frightened to ask quite what she meant about something happening to her, but they nodded. Both were on the verge of tears, but they held them back. Just like their mum, they had to stay strong in front of their younger sisters.

Meanwhile, Hannah Philpott, who never left home without a bottle of holy water, was splashing everyone with it zealously and saying the Hail Mary prayer over and over again. She made them all get on their knees, still wearing their gas masks, and pray to God that He might save them.

'Holy Mary, mother of God, pray for us sinners . . . ' she intoned enthusiastically, as she continued to spray holy water liberally over the frightened party. She was only interrupted when a church warden entered the hall with a puzzled look on his face.

'Not to worry,' he announced. 'It was just a practice alarm.'

Collective jaws dropped inside the gas masks, then a warm wave of relief flooded over them. There were even a few giggles.

There actually was every reason to worry, though. Unbeknown to them, a few minutes before the siren had sounded, the Prime Minister Neville Chamberlain, had made a devastating broadcast to the nation. Speaking from the cabinet room at 10 Downing Street, Chamberlain, who had tried and failed to appease Hitler, had made the fateful announcement that the country was now at war with Germany.

The Jarman sisters had grown up in an unsettled time between the two world wars, when the memories and emotions of those who had lost loved ones during the earlier conflict were still raw. The thought of going through it all again, with husbands and sons being sent off to fight in foreign fields – and the very real possibility of them not returning – was too painful to contemplate.

Pierce had married Ann (Annie) Newland on 21 June 1924,

when they were both thirty, at Most Holy Trinity Church in Dockhead, Bermondsey. It was a thriving Catholic parish, as Dockhead was inhabited predominantly by Irish families or their descendants, like the Jarmans, and there were several Catholic schools. Pierce moved in to Annie's family home – a three-storey terraced Victorian house at 103 Abbey Street – which stood out from others in the street because the front was covered in an impressively verdant Virginia creeper, of which Annie was very proud. Pierce and Annie's first child, Mary, was born on 2 October of that year.

Annie's parents, Tom and Kate, lived on the ground floor with Annie's illiterate brother, Mike, and Kit – the daughter of Annie's sister, also named Kate. Annie's mother had taken Kit into her own care from the age of two, believing she wasn't getting sufficient attention from Annie's sister, who already had a large family by two different men. On the top floor of the house lived Annie's other sister Lylie – a pet corruption of Eliza – and her husband, who the girls knew only as Uncle Dot (none of them knew why), and who had lost a leg during the Great War. After Lylie died in 1926, Dot lived upstairs on his own.

Pierce, Annie and Mary occupied just two rooms on the middle floor – one used as a bedroom; the kitchen in the other – and they would often spend time sitting downstairs with Annie's parents. All of the adults in the house were protective of their private space and everyone was careful not to invade others' rooms. The house itself might have looked quite grand from outside, but there was very little money around for this traditional working-class family and every penny counted.

All of the houses in the neighbourhood, which, in a

previous time, would have been owned by individual families, were now divided up and rented out to various families or individuals. The house next door to the Jarmans, for example, was home to one family downstairs, another on the middle floor and one more on the top floor. At least the Jarmans didn't have to share their home with strangers – they were grateful for that.

However, conditions became ever more cramped for them over the following years as their family increased in size. Two years after the arrival of Mary came their second child, Joan. Three years later, in 1929, came Sheila, followed by Kathleen in 1932 and Patricia in 1933. Five years after that, when Annie was forty-five, she had her last child, Anne.

In the back yard the girls' granddad did his best to create a makeshift garden by growing sunflowers, and the children would marvel at how tall they would get. He had also planted an elderberry tree, which had matured over time. Every year, he gave the abundant crop of berries to Mrs Bradley across the road to make wine. In return, Tom would receive a small glass of elderberry wine as a thank you, which he accepted graciously, although Annie thought it far from generous, suspecting that Mrs Bradley had made bottles of the stuff to enjoy herself or to sell. However, Annie kept her thoughts to herself, as her father seemed quite happy with the neighbourly arrangement.

Living – and particularly sleeping – conditions at 103 Abbey Street were challenging. In their bedroom, Pierce and Annie would have their youngest child in bed with them while their other daughters would top to toe in the other double bed. Each newborn would sleep between Annie and Pierce, which led to some confusion for Mary when, at the age of thirteen, a school friend told her how babies were made.

Mary was shocked and replied in disbelief, 'They can't do that. They have a baby sleeping in the middle of them.'

The girls, including Mary, believed that the midwife brought new babies to their house in the basket on her bicycle because every time they saw her bike they knew they would soon hear a new baby crying!

Annie was always singing around the house – usually hymns – and hankered after owning a piano to accompany her singsongs. Prams were more of a necessity, however, and anyhow, apart from financial concerns, there was a distinct lack of space. Luckily Dot, up on the top floor, did have a piano, which she envied, and she would sneak upstairs while he was at work and play it to her heart's content. Annie had never had any lessons but, although her repertoire was limited, she could certainly knock out a tune. She would start off with 'The Blue Danube', which was usually followed by 'The Skater's Waltz', and would perhaps finish with a hymn, to which she would sing along. Either Mary or Sheila would keep watch downstairs for Uncle Dot's return.

Their uncle moved out eventually and was replaced by a couple named Mr and Mrs Morris. When they left, Pierce, Annie and their brood – with some relief – spread their wings to the top floor, giving them a much-needed extra bedroom, though the increase in council rent was a huge toll on their limited resources.

When Kit moved into her own house after she got married, the girls were excited about getting another bedroom, but Annie – who aspired to the luxuries in life – had other ideas. She had always wanted a nice sitting room, a phrase which sounded very middle class to her and so, despite the lack of money, made monthly instalments on the purchase of a three-piece suite instead, which she thought looked very posh.

'No feet on it,' she would scold her daughters whenever they went near the precious new furniture. Then one day, to the girls' surprise, they returned home from school to find a piano in the sitting room. Now Annie had the freedom to play music whenever and for as long as she wanted . . . or so she imagined. A worried Pierce had cautioned her that money was tight and that they wouldn't be able to keep up with the repayments of 2s 6d per week for the piano on top of those for the suite.

'We're overstretching,' he would say, but he knew that once his wife had set her mind on something it was near impossible to deter her, and so he gave up trying when he realized how much the piano meant to her. He was proved right all too soon, though, when, a few months later, Annie's bursting pride at having a piano delivered in full view of her neighbours was replaced by the shame and sadness she felt at having it taken away equally publicly.

When the van arrived to collect it, the girls, who were playing outside in the street with a skipping rope, were already primed with what to say to their friends. 'Just tell them that it's going to make room for another bed,' Annie had briefed them. They did just that, heads held high, well-versed as they were in the art of keeping up appearances.

Annie thought about all this, now that she was effectively homeless, stranded in a barren church hall far away in Sussex. She missed her familiar surroundings, however cramped and crowded they might have been.

The air-raid panic over, the church hall residents were paid another visit later that morning by the billeting officer. He explained that he was still trying to find them some-where to stay but that they would have to remain where they were until then. Local volunteers brought them more food for lunch, then an evening meal and, although the two mothers were worried about their accommodation, the children were having a delightful time playing in the sunshine in the pretty grounds around the vicarage and church. Annie and Mary Eddicott also walked around outside, trying to enjoy the clean air and the sound of their youngsters' laughter. It was comforting to be with their children and each other.

Once the sun set, the cool of the evening drew in and they all returned inside the hall, which felt soulless, with its bare floorboards and no furnishings other than the camp beds and a trestle table with emergency provisions arranged neatly on top. The girls continued to chatter excitedly as they got into their nightdresses and clambered into their beds, and it was some time before all of the children fell asleep. Annie, however, lay on her own bed and stayed awake for most of the night, wondering just how long they would be in temporary accommodation, how long before they could start to live their lives again.

CHAPTER 2

Battle Road

Pierce (centre left) in the First World War with clasped hands and wearing a hat.

'Good news. We've found you a house,' said the billeting officer with a beaming smile as he arrived at the church hall.

Annie was pleased but apprehensive at the same time. She desperately wanted somewhere to live, but it needed to pass muster.

'Who with?' she asked, barely hidden suspicion in her voice.

'Each other,' came the reply. 'You'll be sharing. The house is empty. It has some furniture there already but we'll sort you out with some extra bits and pieces. It's just a short walk away in Battle Road.'

This was very good news indeed, Annie and Mary decided, and the children were cock-a-hoop. After all the upheaval and anticipation, it was a huge relief to know they would be living with friends rather than strangers.

After packing up their belongings, the two families set off with the billeting officer on a walk that took them past Market Square at the heart of the town, with its council offices, police station and post office, and along the High Street, where they looked through the windows of an array of shops and office buildings, including a tobacconist, newsagent, grocer, fish and chip shop, the grand-looking Grenadier Hotel and the historic Old Court House.

'Everything looks so clean,' Joan said excitedly to Mary. While the girls ogled their new surroundings, taking

33

in the contrast with their dirty corner of London, Annie was acutely aware of curious eyes turned on *them*. She straightened her back and held her head high as she walked with an air of confidence that belied the apprehension and uncertainty she was feeling, so far away from the familiar faces and sights of home.

Turning into Battle Road, which was lined on both sides with terraced Victorian houses, they finally stopped outside number eighteen, where the name plaque beside the front door read 'Heywood'.

'This is it,' said the billeting officer.

From the roadside they took in the red-brick, two-storey house with a bay window at the front and a door, underneath a porch, to the left.

'It looks lovely!' said Kath, suddenly gooey-eyed.

'So pretty,' added Pat.

Even Sheila, who liked pretty things, was starting to think that evacuation was maybe not so bad after all.

Squealing excitedly, the little ones ran through the garden gate, followed by the rest of their families who, having liked the look of the exterior, could hardly wait to see inside. Once through the gate, a path led through the small front garden to the house. From here, another path led down the right side of the house to a side door and continued on to the back garden. There was a raised flowerbed near the side path with a dramatic copper beech tree at its centre.

'The front door is stuck so the previous owner always used the side door,' explained the billeting officer. He led them down the path and, taking the key out of his pocket, unlocked the door, which opened on to a rather bare kitchen, with a cooker, sink and some cupboards.

The most eye-catching 'furniture' in the house was in the modest front room, which was dominated by what looked like a large, rectangular, forbidding metal cage – which is essentially what it was.

'It's enormous!' said Joan, chuckling.

'That's your shelter,' said the billeting officer, less amused. 'To be used whenever you hear the air-raid siren.'

'I don't want to go in there, Mum,' said Pat with a fearful expression on her face. 'It looks horrid.'

Kath reached out and put a protective arm round her little sister, and Annie gave her a reassuring smile.

The Morrison shelter, named after Herbert Morrison, Minister of Home Security, was assembled and bolted together inside the house and measured 6 feet 6 inches long, 4 feet wide and 2 feet 6 inches high, with an entry door through one of the wire-mesh panels. Whilst other shelters, such as the Anderson – named after the Home Secretary, John Anderson – were issued for outside use and made of straight galvanized corrugated steel panels with curved panels for the roof, it was thought that the Morrison's flat top could double as a dining table. However, as the Jarmans were to discover, this was quite impractical because the sides prevented them from tucking their legs underneath. The shelter could accommodate six adults at a squeeze and took up half of the floor space in the front room.

To the rear of the ground floor was a large bedroom with a fine chest of drawers. In the hallway a narrow and rather steep staircase led up to three other bedrooms and a lavatory, which was perched precariously at the top of a steep step so that anyone coming out of it had to make a wide stride to the landing to avoid falling down.

'The thinking is that you and your children, Mrs

Eddicott, would live upstairs,' said the billeting officer. 'The small bedroom at the back can be used as a kitchen. We will get a stove put in. And Mrs Jarman, you would be downstairs with your family.'

The two women looked at each other for a few moments, each thinking the same thing. It would be cramped, but then their homes back in Dockhead were hardly spacious. In any case, they were happy because they had managed to keep their families together as they had vowed.

Annie smiled. 'I think this will suit us fine.'

Downstairs, the children appeared to have already made up their minds that they were going to love it on Battle Road. They had found their way into the back garden and were running around excitedly. This was much more fun than their back yard in Abbey Street, thought the Jarman girls. Here, the garden backed on to fields, which stretched as far as the eye could see.

Kath's face was already alive with wonderment but then she caught sight of something that made her even more wide-eyed.

'Look!' she shouted.

'Where?' replied Pat eagerly, wanting to be let in on her sister's discovery.

'Over there!' said Kath, pointing into the distance.

'I don't see anything,' said Pat.

'Look to where I'm pointing,' said Kath. 'See them?'

Pat squinted until she finally saw the figures. 'What are they?' she asked.

'Cows,' replied Kath, beaming with delight. 'We saw some on the way down on the train, remember?'

Pat looked puzzled. 'What were they doing on the train?'

'They weren't *on* the train. They were out of the window, Pat. In the fields.'

The two sisters ran back inside to tell Annie what they had seen but she and Mary Eddicott were in conversation with the billeting officer, who was explaining that the camp beds from the church hall would be brought into the house for the first few nights until spare beds could be sourced, and that other provisions would be delivered later that day.

'I'll leave you to familiarize yourself with the house for a while and settle in,' he said, as he took his leave in the hallway. 'It will all be more comfortable and homely once you have everything you need.'

They had been given emergency food supplies, which included tins of corned beef, vegetables, bread, tea and orange squash and, while Annie put the kettle on, Mary made some soft drinks for the children. Then they busied themselves with unpacking their meagre possessions in their new home, relieved to have one finally. The past forty-eight hours had felt like an eternity.

That afternoon, there was a knock on the door and Annie opened it to find a small, rotund woman, attired in a grey-and-green woollen jacket, skirt and hat, smiling at her and holding two large laundry bags in either hand. Attached to her jacket lapel was a badge bearing the insignia WVS.

'Good afternoon,' she said cheerfully. 'I'm Mrs Hassen from the Women's Voluntary Service. We help evacuees to settle in here by providing . . . various things.' She looked down at her bags. 'I have some army blankets here for you, along with some sheets.'

'Thank you,' said Annie. 'That's very kind.'

Mrs Hassen smiled warmly. 'And local people and businesses have donated items. Cutlery, crockery, that sort of thing. I'll bring some over later.'

Annie, who had never been offered anything in her life without a price being attached to it, was taken aback and hardly knew what to say. Before she was able to utter anything else, Mrs Hassen, with another little smile, said, 'Nice to meet you,' and turned and walked away, leaving Annie staring after her.

Mary joined her mother at the doorway. 'Is she a nurse, Mum?' she asked.

'No,' said Annie. 'More like our guardian angel at the moment.'

As promised, Mrs Hassen returned later in the day, this time with a troop of boy scouts in tow, who unloaded the camp beds from a truck and set them up in the bedrooms. They also brought with them some dark-green blackout curtains, which they put up over the windows. The girls were unused to having boys in their house and so there was much giggling from the younger ones, who hovered nearby to spy on them before running away when seen . . . and then sneaking back again.

That evening, Annie and Mary Eddicott provided their sprawling families with a meal of cold meat, boiled potatoes and cabbage, which they ate in group rotation at the kitchen table. Shortly afterwards, the excited younger children were put to bed but found it hard to sleep as they lay in their camp beds in this new and strange environment.

'Do you think we'll stay here for ever?' Pat whispered.

'No. Not for ever,' said Kath. 'Well. I don't *think* so.'

'I hope we do,' Pat replied. 'I like it. Do you like it, Kath?'

'Seems all right,' Kath offered.

There was a shuffling sound from a nearby camp bed. 'I'm missing home,' said Sheila.

'But we've only just got here,' said Kath.

'I don't care. It's not home. It's not *our* home. And, besides, Daddy's not here.'

The girls thought about this for a while.

'Do you think Daddy's OK?' Pat asked.

In the excitement of the past two days Kath hadn't given much thought to her father but now she felt a pang of longing. 'I expect so,' she replied eventually.

Downstairs, just as her daughters were whispering about their father, Annie took out a writing pad and a pen from the kitchen drawer and sat at the table to compose a letter.

'Dear Pierce,' she began. And then sat back to gather her thoughts.

The following day was given to settling the children in to the new house before all of them, apart from Mary who had left school that summer, went to their new schools in Hailsham. For Sheila, Kath and Pat this was a temporary classroom set up in the village hall for evacuees of primary-school age while proper arrangements were made for them to attend the local school. The classes were run by Miss Mobbs and another teacher from a school in Rotherhithe, Miss Hey-wood, who had travelled to Hailsham with their pupils.

Although they only had to attend the makeshift school for a few hours in the morning, the Jarman sisters took an instant dislike to head teacher Miss Mobbs, who they thought was overly stern. Nevertheless, Kath and Pat mucked in and made the best of things, but Sheila was feeling so homesick that the morning seemed to drag until she was finally free to be back with her mother.

'It will get better. You'll see. It just takes a bit of getting used to because it's all new to you,' said Annie, as she poured Sheila some orange squash in the kitchen.

Sheila had her doubts, though. Having always loved reading and writing, she sat down to write a song about their new abode, choosing neutral lyrics that didn't give any indication of her feelings, which she was trying hard to keep hidden. She sang it to a simple tune she had composed herself, and it proved to be so catchy that her sisters would also sing it on a regular basis during that first year in Sussex.

Heywood, 18 Battle Road, Heywood, 18 Battle Road.
For the present
We are living in
Heywood, 18 Battle Road.

However, as time went on 'the present' seemed increasingly like 'for ever'. Until the tide of war slowly started to change.

Joan was having a similarly hard time settling in. Now aged twelve, she began to attend the secondary school almost opposite their house in Battle Road. Hailsham Senior Mixed was quite different to Joan's previous experience of school. Having come from a Catholic girls' school in Bermondsey, where she had been taught exclusively by nuns, she found it difficult to adapt to being in a class with boys and to being taught by men. To make matters worse, she formed an instant crush on her teacher, Mr Nichols, who she thought was one of the most handsome men she had ever seen – despite his thick, horn-rimmed glasses.

Joan was especially conscious that she and her sisters sounded very different from the local children of Hailsham – who the Jarman girls considered to be 'posh' – and didn't find it easy fitting in at school. She also felt that some of her classmates were snobs and treated her shabbily. It was good news, then, that Mr Nichols took a shine to Joan – realizing how hard it must be for her as an evacuee in a new school. It was clear that he wanted to help and encourage her as much as he could.

It still wasn't plain sailing, though – and at times it was downright disastrous. Joan had always thought she was good at mental arithmetic – addition, subtraction, division and multiplication was what she was used to – but to her horror, her new class was working on fractions and percentages, which she hadn't yet studied at all.

One day in class, they were given a quick test. As Mr Nichols read out each question, the pupils wrote down their answers in their exercise books. Joan became increasingly anxious when one question after another passed and she had no idea what the answer was. In a panic, she began scribbling figures down in the hope that *something* might be right, but by the time she had finished she felt sick with worry and nerves.

'Right. Swap your books with whoever's next to you and when I call out the answers, tick the ones that are correct and put a cross against the incorrect ones,' said Mr Nichols.

Joan felt her heart sink even further. Now she was going to be publicly humiliated. She toyed with the idea of not handing over her exercise book but the girl next to her was already proffering hers and so Joan swapped reluctantly. As Mr Nichols read out the answers, Joan began to feel worse and worse as she made one tick after another on her neighbour's page. When she was passed her own book back and saw a cross against every single one of her answers, she felt so ashamed that she wanted to cry.

'Which clever person got them all right? Twenty out of twenty?' Mr Nichols asked with a smile. A couple of hands shot up proudly.

'Excellent. Well done. Nineteen?' A few more hands went up. As he counted his way down, Joan felt that she would rather be anywhere than here.

'Five? Four?'

Panic rising, Joan was sure that she would be the only one who had not got any right at all.

'Two? One?'

In a desperate attempt to avoid complete humiliation, she put her hand up.

'OK, Joan. I'll work on those with you and you'll soon get the hang of things,' Mr Nichols said kindly.

Then came the not-so-kind remark from the girl who had marked Joan's score and knew *exactly* how many she had got right. In a loud voice she said, 'She didn't get anything, sir!'

Joan felt her face flush with embarrassment but Mr Nichols ignored the comment, which filled her with relief and made her teacher even more admirable in her eyes.

When Joan arrived home from school, Annie asked her how her day had been.

'The kids are snobby and maths is nothing like what we did in Dockhead,' she replied miserably.

'And your teacher?' asked Annie.

Battle Road

'Oh, Mum!' said Joan, her eyes widening and a smile creeping on to her face. 'He looks just like Errol Flynn!'

The girls made the most of the garden in their first few days at Battle Road. The freedom of open space all around them was a completely new feeling, and they knew they were very privileged to have some grassland where they could sit or play right outside their own house.

Back in London, despite their granddad's best efforts in the back yard, the play area was the road and they would spend every spare hour in the street with their friends. It was quite safe as there were seldom any cars, just horses and carts and the occasional lorry. One of their favourite pastimes was to lay a long, thick dray rope across the road, with two girls each holding an end in both hands. They would slowly begin to swing it, building momentum until, when the moment was judged exactly right, a group of their friends would rush into the middle and begin to skip along to one of their favourite skipping songs. Indeed, there were so many songs that they even had them for special occasions: 'Good Fri-day, never let the rope go emp-ty.'

Should any horse and cart or vehicle come into the road, the rope would be lowered to the floor to let it pass over and then the game would continue.

There was also a peculiar little ditty for consecutively throwing and catching two or three balls at the wall.

> One, two, three, O'Leary,
> My ball's down the airy,
> Give it to Jane and not to Mary
> Outside the penny bazaar.

Another much-loved game was whip and top, and the girls particularly liked to coil the whip around the spinning top, stick the point of the top into the nearest piece of earth, usually at the bottom of a tree, and cover it with some silver foil. Once the whip was pulled away sharply, the top would spin in place and delight the children with the dazzling silver glare. They would also amuse themselves by seeing who could keep a large wooden hoop rolling the longest by hitting it from behind with a stick.

In Battle Road the Jarman sisters, unused to playing anywhere else, naturally took to skipping outside the house. It was a particular favourite pastime of Sheila's, who could go on for hours without tiring. During their games early one evening, a man who lived two doors along the road approached them with a look of disapproval on his face. Joan recognized him as one of her teachers.

'I don't think you should be playing in the street,' he said to the girls. 'Why don't you go into the garden and play?'

'We've always played in the street,' said Joan.

'Well, we don't play in the street here,' he replied brusquely, and walked off.

The girls looked at each other, feeling the force of his rebuke, and with all the fun having vanished in an instant, they trooped back inside the house, feeling oddly ashamed. From then on they played either in the garden or in the nearby recreation ground, known as the rec. It was another reminder that they were different; that their London ways were not necessarily welcome in Hailsham.

The Thursday of that first week in Battle Road, Pat turned six. Before setting off for school, her sisters wished her a happy birthday and gave her cards. So too did Annie, writing 'Love from Mum and Dad' inside, complete with kisses, even though Pierce was miles away. It was the first time that he had ever missed being there for one of his daughters' birthdays and his absence was felt keenly by all. A smiling Pat just had time to open presents, which included crayons and sweets, before leaving for school but she looked dejected when Annie told her there would be no cake that evening. She cheered up instantly, however, when Annie added, 'We'll save that for the weekend, when Daddy comes down.'

During that first week, the girls looked forward eagerly to the arrival of their father and the chance to tell him all their news. Meanwhile, Annie determined to make the new house feel like a home once some extra furniture and provisions arrived. Upstairs, Mary Eddicott did the same for her family, feeling that things were looking up after a stove was installed and she was able to cook a proper hot meal.

Pierce had written back to Annie to say that he would visit them on Friday evening after work and stay with them over the weekend before travelling back to London on Sunday evening. Annie had given him instructions, as best she could, to take a train to Polegate, then a bus to Hailsham and a short walk to Battle Road, but she felt very far away from London and worried all week that he wouldn't be able to find them. While the younger girls were all at school on Friday, Mary helped Annie make one of Pierce's favourite meat pies for him to enjoy with his family on his arrival.

Although she missed him terribly, Annie was comforted by the thought that Pierce was not entirely on his own at home. As well as having her parents living downstairs, Pierce's spinster sisters, Nell, Rose and Mary, who lived nearby in Stanworth Street, were very protective towards their brother. Annie had no doubt that he would be spending many evenings at their house where they would spoil him with their home cooking and feed him luxuries he could barely afford when she was in charge of the family meals.

Pierce's sisters were rather stern and forbidding. Not only did they share a house, but they also all worked together as machinists – making army uniforms once the war started – and they were a formidable team who doted on their brother. Annie had never got on with them very well and was convinced that their frostiness stemmed from their resentment towards Annie for taking their brother away by marrying him.

At least living here in Hailsham I'll be well away from them, she thought to herself as she rolled out the pastry for Pierce's pie.

The girls too were less than fond of their aunts. The women had no affinity with children and lacked any of the warmth or kindness that might be expected from an aunt, being more of the 'children should be seen and not heard' school of family relations. At least they shared a love of Pierce and, as Friday evening drew on, the girls looked forward excitedly to seeing their father. Kath, Sheila and Pat twittered on.

'When will he be here, Mum?'

'What time?'

'How long now?'

'Girls, you're getting under my feet,' said Annie, putting the pie in the oven whilst Mary and Joan helped to prepare the vegetables. 'Why don't you go and look out of the window and watch for him?'

'Yes!' they squealed and scampered off.

At first, they stared intently out of the window, thinking every passer-by was Daddy.

'There he is!' said Kath. 'Oh, no . . . *That's* him! Oh, wait a minute . . . No.'

'Is *that* him?' asked Pat.

'Course not, Pat. Don't be silly.'

After a while, Sheila tired of looking out of the window and went off to help out in the kitchen. Kath and Pat were thinking of giving up too, when they saw him appear.

'He's here! He's here! Daddy's here!' they yelled. As Annie and the older girls joined them from the kitchen, they watched the familiar figure, brown holdall in hand and flat cap on head, studying the front door of each house as he approached.

Annie rushed out to meet him, reaching out and embracing him tightly. 'I'm not sure they do that in the street here,' she said, smiling.

'Eh?'

'Never mind. You're late,' she teased. 'Tea's ready.'

They walked arm in arm towards the house but didn't get very far as the girls rushed out to welcome him 'home'.

Pierce barely had time to put his bag down in the hallway before he was dragged around the house, from room to room, by his excitable daughters, who were eager to show him their new surroundings. Like the girls, he thought the garden lovely. He felt a surge of relief and happiness that they were all together as one, living in a nice house and had been looked after. The feeling threatened to overwhelm him.

'I've missed you all . . . so much,' he said with a tear in his eye, suddenly overcome with emotion.

Annie watched him, smiling sympathetically, as the girls chorused, 'We missed you too, Daddy.'

'The girls have so much to tell you,' Annie said to her husband. 'But they can do that over tea.'

During the meal, Pierce listened attentively to their stories, interjecting with the odd question about school, friends and life in Hailsham.

'All the kids are snooty,' said Joan. 'They don't like us much. They're not very nice at school.'

'They're not very nice at the rec, either,' piped up Kath. 'Calling us names like "ginger".'

'Yeah,' added Pat, feeling that she should contribute something to the string of complaints.

Pierce looked over at Sheila, who had been unusually quiet. 'How are you finding things, Sheila?'

'Oh, it's all right, I suppose,' she said. 'But I miss my friends from back home. And we all miss you.'

Pierce gave a little smile. 'Well, I miss you all too. Lots,' he replied.

When they'd cleared their plates, Annie asked the girls to sit around the table a little longer, and she fetched a home-baked cake from the larder with six candles burning in a circle. Pat glowed with pleasure as Pierce led the chorus of 'Happy Birthday' and told her to make a wish. Screwing up her eyes, and puffing out her cheeks, she silently wished that her father could live with them for ever. Then she blew with all her might until the last of the flickering flames went out.

After slices of cake and much laughter, the younger girls went off to play while Mary and Joan cleared the table and started the washing-up. Pierce and Annie stayed seated, relishing each other's company once more.

'And how have *you* been coping?' Annie asked him.

'I've been managing,' he said.

'I expect you've been spending most evenings in the pub. While the cat's away . . . '

'No . . . no,' Pierce protested. Then, with a shy smile he added, 'Well, I've had one or two pints. But . . . no.'

'Yes, I can imagine.' Annie gave him a knowing look. 'Have you seen much of your sisters?' she continued airily.

She wasn't in the slightest bit surprised when he said that they had been cooking for him, but his next comment did startle her. 'They thought that they might like to visit.'

Horror flashed across Annie's face and, seeing it, Pierce quickly added, 'After a while. Not yet.'

'But we can't put them up here,' Annie protested. 'There's barely enough room for *us*.'

'Oh, they can stay somewhere nearby,' Pierce replied. 'They're not short of a bob, after all.'

'I know that!' said Annie sharply, but not wanting to ruin the moment she then fell silent. She was used to getting her own way most of the time but knew when to withdraw tactfully.

Later that evening, with the washing-up done, the family settled in the front room and the girls were delighted when Pierce reached for his bag and brought out some of their toys and books from home, which they hadn't had room for in their own bags to bring themselves. With such familiar items in the house it began to feel more like a proper home.

After the girls had gone to bed, Pierce and Annie chatted some more and gave each other a kiss and a cuddle before retiring for the night. There wasn't much room for any more romance as Annie crept into the one remaining camp bed in the bedroom full of her sleeping daughters while Pierce huddled down on the living-room sofa.

The following day saw the Jarman family strolling around Hailsham, with Annie pushing three-month old Anne in her pram, and the other girls showing Pierce the local landmarks.

'That's my school,' Joan pointed out. 'There's a really nice teacher there. Mr Nichols. Teaches maths.'

An amused Annie commented, 'Looks just like Errol Flynn, apparently.'

'Errol Flynn,' repeated a smiling Pierce. 'Well, I bet he's popular.'

As they turned into the High Street, they walked through the historic market square and then turned right into George Street where Pierce was directed to marvel at the ornate, neo-classical design of the gleaming-white Pavilion Cinema. In truth, though, his eye was more attracted to the cosy, inviting lure of the nearby George Inn.

They showed Pierce the vicarage and church hall where they had been taken on the day of their evacuation and then took a leisurely walk around the large pond on the common in the centre of town.

On Sunday morning, with the children at church, Pierce walked down to the newsagent to buy the *News of the World*, his newspaper of choice, and sat down on a chair in the front room to read about how war was escalating overseas. Canada had joined Britain, France, Australia and New Zealand in declaring war on Germany, and the War Cabinet warned that the conflict would be long but it would be victory at all costs. Pierce felt stirred by the confidence and patriotism but the

German military and naval build-up was increasing at an alarming rate.

After church, on that sunny, balmy afternoon, as the girls sat in the garden, chatting and casually picking and eating the loganberries that were poking through the fence of the adjoining garden, international hostility seemed to be happening in another world.

'Don't eat too many. You'll get a bad tummy,' Mary advised her sisters, as she stretched out her legs.

Joan gave one of the protruding branches a tug. 'We've not had many,' she said.

Suddenly, they were startled by the appearance of a head over the fence. It belonged to a tall and slim woman with iron-grey hair pulled into a bun, and she was frowning.

'You may have any berries that are on your side of the fence but don't pull any through,' she said sternly.

The girls felt very guilty as the woman turned away but then decided that she had been unnecessarily harsh on them.

'She's a bit mean,' whispered Kath. 'There's loads of fruit in her garden. Wouldn't you think she would let us have some?'

'A real meanie,' Pat agreed.

When the girls told Annie what had happened, Annie remarked that she had already met their neighbour.

'She seemed very kind,' she insisted. 'She's called Mrs Goldsmith and she's a nurse. She promised to give me an old highchair for Anne when she needs it, so don't go disrespecting her. Remember it's *us* who have to fit in here. Not everyone is happy to have evacuees moving in. And she lives on her own so she's not used to having people around.'

The girls were a little surprised to hear their mother,

always fiercely protective of her daughters, sticking up for someone she hardly knew. But because of this they took her caution to heart.

Overhearing the conversation, Pierce thought how lonely life must be not to have a loving family around you. After Annie and his daughters were evacuated he had enjoyed one or two peaceful moments when he knew he could just relax at home and not be bothered or answerable to anyone, but the novelty was fleeting and he'd frequently sought out his sisters for company that week.

That evening, he and Annie were in a melancholy mood as he packed his bag in the bedroom and prepared to leave his family once more to return to Bermondsey.

'This just all seems so strange,' said Annie.

'Yes, and I can't see things changing any time soon,' he replied.

'Will you be OK?' Annie asked.

Pierce smiled. '*I'm* fine. It's you and the girls I'm worried about.'

'It's a different life but I have to say, I do feel safer here,' said Annie.

Pierce leant over to kiss her gently. Back downstairs, he hugged and kissed his family in an echo of the scene a week earlier on the doorstep of 103 Abbey Street.

'I'll be back down next Friday, now that I've found you.' He smiled. 'Be good for Mummy, everyone,' he added, glancing quickly at Kath. With a final kiss for Annie he departed, waved off by his family at the garden gate. And, once more, he felt a lump in his throat.

Annie's advice to her daughters about trying to fit in with the locals was put to the test a couple of days later when

Kath decided to fight fire with fire. She was walking along Battle Road with Pat on their way into town. As they passed the junction with North Street, a group of local girls started chanting a song that dated back to before the Great War.

> Ginger, you're barmy,
> You ought to join the army.
> You'll get knocked out by a bottle of stout,
> Ginger, you're barmy.

The two sisters felt very frightened and Pat snuggled up close behind Kath for protection. Although Kath wasn't feeling very protective she made an instant decision to brazen it out, come what may.

'Let's run, Kath!' urged Pat.

'No,' said Kath, with a steely look and clenched fists. 'We're not running from anyone. Mum has always told us to stick up for ourselves.'

One of the girls stepped into the middle of the pavement, blocking their path. In response, Kath rolled up her sleeves theatrically in an unmistakeable show of getting ready for a fight.

'Here. Hold my hanky,' she said to Pat – she didn't have a coat, so this was the best she could do – and proceeded to pass her sister the scrunched-up kerchief that had been festering inside her sleeve. Pat took it like a boxing trainer being passed his fighter's robe.

To Kath's amazement, as she approached the lead girl, the girl turned and fled, closely followed by the others. Kath couldn't quite believe it. Her heart was thumping with nerves but her chest was pumped up with pride. She had seen them off and she continued the walk into town with something of a swagger in her step, while Pat shot glances of pure admiration up at her heroic sister.

Over at the rec the Jarman sisters encountered further hostility, during their early days in Hailsham, from local girls who objected to them playing on the swings, roundabout and slide. One girl, who had obviously been listening to her parents, told Joan haughtily, 'You shouldn't be playing here. It's for the people of Hailsham. We pay our rates and taxes.' In contrast, most of the boys were more than happy to have a new girl around, although Joan was a little young to have figured out why.

The rec also became a regular haunt for Annie during the afternoons. She would push Anne there in her pram and sit with the other evacuee mums from London for a chat. Once a week a military band performed at the bandstand, playing popular tunes such as 'Sussex By The Sea', and they would always end with the national anthem. If the band expected the mothers to be patriotic and stand in traditional fashion at that point, then they were disappointed because as soon as the anthem began the women took it as a signal that the musical performance was over and it was time to go home. The conductor would triumphantly lead the band through an impressive crescendo to the final resounding chord and turn for applause with gusto, only to see that the audience had gone!

A local woman, a spinster who lived with her father, regularly took a walk through the rec and would stop to listen to the band. She would smile and say hello to the mothers, and to Annie in particular. After a while, the two women started engaging in lively conversation and the lady was very interested to hear about the Jarmans' life in

London and their experience as evacuees. A kindly if rather lonely soul, she arrived at the house on Battle Road one day with a pie that she had made for the family. Annie was touched by her act and called the girls into the kitchen to introduce them to Miss Hunt.

Miss Hunt was dressed in black, as usual, with striking steel-grey hair and a pale face, which made the girls imagine she was very old indeed, although she was probably little older than their mother.

'Miss Hunt has very kindly cooked a pie for us, girls. Isn't that lovely?' said Annie.

The girls thanked Miss Hunt enthusiastically and she left with a smile on her face, seemingly pleased to be cooking for more than just herself and her father for a change. Now others would be able to appreciate her culinary skills. Unfortunately, although the family appreciated her kindness, the same could not be said when it came to the pie.

'We can't eat this, Mum,' Joan said to Annie as she sliced into it. 'The pastry hasn't been made or cooked properly. It's still very pale. And the meat doesn't look right.'

Annie came over and agreed that it looked unappetizing and was probably inedible. After poking it for a bit and trying a morsel, she reluctantly – because she hated waste – threw it in the bin.

'Can't we give the pastry to the birds, Mum?' Sheila asked.

Annie screwed up her face. 'I wouldn't want to poison them,' she replied, making the girls giggle.

A couple of days later, as she was pushing Anne in her pram at the rec, Annie met Miss Hunt again.

'How did you enjoy the pie?' asked Miss Hunt.

'Oh, lovely. Thank you so much,' said Annie.

'The girls ate it all up?'

'There wasn't a scrap to be seen,' said Annie, with an element of truth.

Miss Hunt beamed. 'I'll make some cakes next time,' she said.

Annie forced a little smile. 'Please don't put yourself to any trouble. You've been more than generous. You really shouldn't.'

Miss Hunt held up a restraining hand. 'I want to. It's my pleasure.'

Sadly the pleasure was hers alone as her regular deliveries of cakes and pies to Battle Road were dumped in the bin unceremoniously as soon as she had left.

Mrs Hassen, from the WVS, was also a regular visitor to the house. Each week she arrived to ask if the family had all they needed. Annie, taking advantage of her kindness, managed to convince her that they had one less blanket than Mrs Hassen thought. This scam worked successfully on a couple of occasions before Annie decided not to press her luck any further. Now she would have two spare blankets to take home with her once war was over. But that would be some time in the future. For now Annie and her girls had to get used to life in Hailsham.

Evenings on the residential street were deathly quiet and pitch black, with only the occasional hoot of an owl or bark of a dog to break the silence. It was a far cry from the streets of Bermondsey, where the locals were out and about until pub closing time.

Saturday nights in Dockhead were particularly raucous. At around ten o'clock, the girls would watch from their bedroom window to see the local characters returning from the pubs. Amongst them were close neighbours Mr Jeffries and Mr Beecham – best pals during the week, fighting foes once they got a few beers down them at the weekend. Luckily, they were always so drink-sodden they rarely managed to land a punch on each other, which the girls found endlessly hilarious. Then there was Mrs Pacey. Every Saturday, she would stagger up the street singing 'On Moonlight Bay'. She would take three steps forward and two steps back, all the way home, invariably with a policeman walking behind her to see that she didn't come to any harm.

Those antics seemed far away now, as Saturday nights in Battle Road were just as peaceful as any other night of the week. Sunday evenings saw all the girls quite subdued following the departure of their father as he made his way back to London, and they knew that the week ahead would seem like an eternity until he returned. Each night in bed, Sheila would hear her sisters gently snoring as she lay awake, picturing him arriving at the familiar house in Abbey Street, which she sorely missed. She wished, more than anything, that she'd been able to travel home with him, holding his hand.

CHAPTER 3

Fitting In

Annie with Anne, aged about eighteen months.

MARY TURNED FIFTEEN on 2 October 1939, and she and Annie decided it was time for her to look for a job. The extra income would be a welcome boost to the household and Mary, like her parents, had a strong work ethic, so was eager to start earning her own money once more.

Back in Bermondsey, Mary had left school at the age of fourteen to get a job. Annie had taught all of her daughters how to cook, sew and knit, and they also had homemaking lessons at school. Mary had been particularly good with a needle and thread, and enjoyed making clothes for herself and for her sisters, so dressmaking seemed a natural choice of career.

As Mary prepared to leave school, the head teacher had arranged for her and a few other girls to visit a labour exchange in Great Portland Street, in London's West End, where Mary was told that Koupy Gowns was looking for a trainee machinist. Koupy, named after its American owner Charles Kuperstein, was an upmarket dress manufacturer situated in Poland Street, just off Oxford Street, the thriving hub of London's shopping scene.

On the day of her interview, Mary had been excited but nervous, tripping over her words as she answered questions about her previous sewing experience. She was so sure her nerves had scuppered her chances that she couldn't believe it when they offered her the job.

At Koupy, Mary had looked enviously at the beautiful dresses, which were sold in prestigious stores such as Harvey Nichols, and dreamt that one day she might get to wear one herself.

'It's really posh, Mum,' she'd told Annie after her first day at work. 'The dresses are beautiful. Made of such lovely material.'

Mary was taught how to use a sewing machine and follow patterns, and gradually got used to working with the luxurious silks, satins and crêpes, learning how to make neat, professional seams. She loved to handle the glamorous day dresses, with their puffed sleeves, calf-length flowing skirts and belted waists which were so fashionable amongst the wealthier women of London.

Her favourite moments, though, were when she was allowed to help dress the mannequins in the showroom. That was when she could daydream. As she handled each smooth silk gown and fastened it around the mannequin, Mary imagined that the slim, static figure was a glamorous film star and that she was her personal dresser.

Another of her tasks had been going out to buy Mr Kuperstein's lunch every day. Although it was menial, she enjoyed this too because it provided a break and her boss would also give her a treat.

'Buy yourself an ice-cream with the change,' he'd said to her on her first day. From then on she would regularly give herself treats of either ice-cream, cake or sweets while out on the lunchtime errand.

Mary had liked Mr Kuperstein who, in turn, found her youth and cockney accent charming, and would make a fuss of her whenever he saw her. 'How are you today, Mary?' he would ask. 'Enjoying it here? You know, back in the States you would still be at school. They start them so young here.'

Mary had been very happy to be at work, though. She'd learnt all she needed to know to make a good fist of life. She was paid 12 shillings per week and gave it all to her mother as soon as she got home every Friday. Annie would promptly give her 2 shillings back for pocket money, which Mary would use to go to the cinema with a friend, buy an ice-cream and also a pair of stockings.

She'd had to resign from her job once the evacuation process started and Annie had needed her eldest daughter to be a child once more so that she could be evacuated with her sisters. Annie had gone back to Mary's school and asked the headmistress, Sister Francis, if she would put Mary back on the school register, and Sister Francis was happy to oblige. Now Mary was settled in Hailsham, though, she had to put her thoughts once more to getting work.

The biggest employer in Hailsham was Green Brothers factory in Summerheath Road. The company had an excellent reputation for their skilled workforce and standard of product. They made high-quality ropes, including those used by the hangman, sail cloth, high-quality garden furniture and camping equipment. As part of the war effort they had also diversified into making sand bags: for the troops on the front line to provide protective barriers, and also on the home front to be stacked along the walls of important buildings, such as the War Office, police stations and schools, for additional protection from bomb explosions.

Green Brothers' war effort far exceeded the manufacture of sand bags, however. In November 1939, they were given a top-secret contract to construct, in kit form, hundreds of dummy Hurricane fighter planes made of wood and canvas, which were deployed across the country on decoy airfields to mislead enemy bombers. A real Hurricane cost between £4,000 and £5,000 but these dummy ones were just £50 each.

It was Annie who had noticed a sign outside the Green Brothers premises, advertising for factory hands, and she suggested to Mary that she should give it a try. Mary, who had had a taste of glamour and sophistication at Koupy Gowns, was not exactly enamoured with the idea.

'I don't know about factory work, Mum,' she said.

'We're not in London any more, Mary,' Annie reminded her. 'You can't be as choosy here. There aren't so many jobs. Why don't you go for it and see what happens? Even if it's just a temporary measure.'

The following day, Mary, in her freshly washed and ironed dress, walked down to the factory gates, where she asked to speak to the foreman. After asking Mary about her life in London, the foreman was impressed by her experience as a machinist and was happy to try her out.

On her first day, Annie kissed her daughter goodbye and Mary took the short walk to Green Brothers. It was a large, red-brick building and, making her way through the tall, arched metal gates at the entrance, Mary wondered what this new chapter in her life would bring. In the event, it turned out to be less of a chapter and more of a half-finished sentence . . .

After reporting to the foreman, Mary was shown to the factory floor where there were stacks of old sacks piled almost to the ceiling, ready to be made into sandbags. The stench of manure emanating from them was overpowering and each time one of the factory workers pulled out a sack, prior to cutting and stitching it to size, it sent yet another haze of thick, pungent dust swirling around, making Mary choke and feel nauseous. The foreman stood with Mary as she watched how the other women were making the sandbags and, after he left, Mary carefully pulled out an old sack to work on. She tried not to disturb the dust too much and, at the same time, hold her breath but with everyone else working around her, it wasn't long before she was covered in filth.

It was a morning of dirty, unpleasant work and a deeply depressed Mary was relieved to get out and breathe the fresh air at lunchtime. She walked home quickly to get a bite to eat.

'What on earth do you look like?' asked a shocked Annie when Mary walked through the door, covered in dust and grime and reeking to high heaven.

'Oh, Mum, it's disgusting. The sacks are all old and stinky. You can smell manure on them. It's horrid,' Mary blurted out. She began to cry at the thought of returning but, to Mary's surprise, Annie had no intention of making her go back to the factory.

'I'm not having that,' said Annie, appalled that one of her girls should be put to work doing such a dirty job. 'You're not going back. You're a dressmaker who has worked with luxury gowns in the West End.'

Mary felt relieved but worried. 'But they'll be expecting me,' she said.

'They can expect on,' retorted Annie.

'But I'll have to tell them.'

'You can pop back in the morning and let them know.'

'Oh, Mum, I don't want to,' Mary whined.

'You mean you want to carry on working there?'

'No. I don't, but . . . '

'Would you like me to come with you?' Annie asked.

Mary nodded. 'But you won't make a scene, will you, Mum?' she said, only too aware of her mother's temper and that familiar flash of anger in her eyes.

'No, I won't make a scene. Now go and have a good wash. You smell like a pig farm.'

The following morning Annie didn't have much to say on their walk to Greens, which made Mary feel even more uneasy.

'You won't start shouting, will you, Mum?' she asked.

'I'll be perfectly calm. Don't worry. You can do the talking.'

The pair walked into the factory – Mary miserably and Annie defiantly – and Annie asked one of the workers for the foreman. After a few minutes' wait, he appeared and ushered them into an office.

'I don't think the job is right for me. I'm sorry but I don't want to work here any longer,' a nervous Mary mumbled.

'What's wrong with it?' he asked.

'What's *wrong* with it?' interjected Annie fiercely, the words flying out of her mouth. 'I was shocked when I saw the state of her yesterday lunchtime. That's no job for a fifteen-year-old girl to do, working in dirt.'

The foreman looked at her for a moment and sneered. 'I thought that coming from London, you'd be used to being in dirty conditions.'

Annie felt like slapping him. 'Bloody cheek!' she stormed. 'We don't live in shit!'

'Come on, Mum,' said Mary, grabbing her arm, and attempting to pull her away.

Annie stared at the foreman, eyes blazing. 'You owe her half a day's pay,' she said.

Fitting In

And so, with that paltry amount of money in hand, Mary and Annie walked out of the compound, never to return.

Annie's retort to the foreman might have been colourful but she did have a point. Their home in London was cramped and they had little money for the nice things in life but she made the most of what they had and everything in the house was kept immaculately clean.

The three oldest girls all had weekly chores, which included washing the linoleum on two flights of stairs and then polishing the brass stair rods until they gleamed, and mopping the hallway as well as the front doorstep. Like most of the neighbours, they even cleaned the pavement outside their house, either using a pumice stone and plenty of water, or dissolving some Vim scouring powder in a bucket of water and scrubbing a half-moon shape on the slabs. This was a weekly ritual and an outward show of standards. The underlying message was that money might be tight but theirs was a clean and respectable house. Anyone who didn't keep this important outside area spotless was frowned upon.

Mary had also been taught housewifery at school – how to clean windows, wash and dry dishes, and wash and iron clothes, including dry cleaning with white spirit. Mary took her coat to school to be cleaned in this way and was delighted with the result. She even got to prepare for motherhood by practising on a baby doll, washing and dressing her and laying her to sleep in a cot. Mary was a grafter, though – she wanted to be more than just a mum. She really wanted to work and she knew how important the extra money was to her large family.

Shortly after the sand-bag disaster Mary saw a job

advertised in Baker's sweet shop, just off the High Street. They were looking for a shop assistant. Mary liked this store – as did all the children in the neighbourhood. The shop window was full of inviting sweets – lemon sherbets, flying saucers, liquorice, milk bottles, humbugs, peppermints – and inside, on the shelves, were jars and jars of more of the same, along with an ice-cream counter.

Mrs Baker, a tall, willowy woman, took Mary on, working afternoons until another girl would take over once she had finished school. The job didn't pay much and Mary knew it was only temporary, but she loved it. She and her sisters had never had many treats in life and working in the shop was like walking into Aladdin's Cave, with row upon row of colourful temptations. Mary's mouth watered at the sights and smells of the wonderful store.

Mrs Baker had a daughter, Eileen, who was ten years older than Mary, and mother and daughter would regularly go into nearby Eastbourne for an afternoon, leaving Mary in charge. She liked those times best of all – particularly as she occasionally helped herself to a sweet or a scoop of ice-cream. The temptation was overpowering and, although she kept telling herself not to give in, resistance was a trial. She was careful never to take too many sweets, though. Having trusted her to look after the shop, Mary felt a duty to Mrs Baker and felt guilty in betraying that trust.

Meanwhile, the war seemed rather quiet as far as Britain was concerned, despite the passing into law of the National Service Act, which called the country's young men for conscription into the armed forces. Both Pierce and Annie thanked God that, unlike many of their friends, they were spared the gut-churning experience of seeing their sons signing up.

However, in the first eight months of the conflict – later to be known as the Phoney War – there was no major military operation on the Western Front. Bombs were not raining down on Britain as feared either, and many began to believe that things were not as grave as they had sounded. They even questioned the necessity of evacuation, thinking it had been an over-reaction. A familiar phrase passed between neighbours in the cities as well as in rural areas such as Hailsham was, 'It will all be over by Christmas'. Some parents even decided to take their children back home to London with them.

The Government responded. In London, on his way to and from work, Pierce began to see new posters from the Ministry of Health pasted to the hoardings. They used less than subtle scare tactics to target those thinking of bringing their children back to the city. One depicted a mother playing with her children in the countryside whilst, standing over her shoulder, the ghostly spectre of Hitler whispers in her ear, 'Take them back! Take them back! Take them back!' as he points to London being bombed in the distance. Underneath, in big type, was the message, 'Don't do it, Mother – leave the children where they are.'

Christmas came and went, and January 1940 was one of the coldest months on record in Hailsham and Eastbourne. At 18 Battle Road the blackout curtains were pulled closely together as usual at night but, stepping out into the dark to look at the snowy landscape that stretched from the end of the garden into the fields in the distance, Mary marvelled at how it was all lit up under the glow of the moon so that you could see for miles. If any German planes were crossing the Channel, the gleaming snow would act as a shining beacon, guiding them in, Mary thought to herself. Still, there was nothing anyone could do about that.

The girls loved playing in the thick snow, either in their garden or at the rec, making snowmen and throwing snowballs at each other. They had never seen anything like this in London, where any snowfall turned quickly to a dirty grey mush as it was trodden underfoot. Here, it was of the crisp and gleaming-white type depicted on Christmas cards and in festive Hollywood movies.

The most tangible sign on the home front that the war was hotting up and things were becoming difficult, was that food was becoming less available. Lurking German U-boats were cutting off the supply chain of food carried by merchant ships into Britain. To ensure the fair distribution of supplies amongst the population, the Ministry of Food issued ration books to every person in the country. Bacon, butter and sugar were the first foodstuffs to be restricted on 8 January 1940 – well and truly signalling the end of the festive period. All other meats were rationed two months later, followed by fish, jam, biscuits, breakfast cereals, cheese, eggs, milk and canned fruit.

The Ministry of Food began to issue weekly leaflets entitled 'Food Facts', containing recipes and advice on how to make a little go a long way, which was just what Annie required for her brood. One leaflet, headed 'Soup for Air Raids', advised, 'Try to make soup every day so you always have some ready to heat up. A hot drink works wonders at a time of shock or strain.' There was also a daily broadcast on the wireless every morning at 8.15 a.m., aimed at helping housewives become increasingly inventive in the kitchen.

Fitting In

Annie did not always have the money to buy a joint of meat for a Sunday roast but when she did, she made the most of it the day after by following a recipe called 'Monday Pie', which used leftovers to make another nutritious meal. Stews, which also used up any scraps of meat, were regularly on the hob in the Jarman kitchen, as they were in many homes up and down the country.

The Women's Institute was at the forefront of the drive to increase food production at home, and the growing of vegetables in the garden at home was encouraged. Not that Annie had much idea about how to grow vegetables; they had always come from the shop back in London. Nevertheless, Annie often gazed at her garden and wondered what she could do with it and how she could do her bit.

In a certain patch, there grew what she thought were daffodils.

'They'll be lovely when they come out in the spring,' she told the girls. However, as the spring of 1940 went on and the daffodil stalks grew taller and taller, Annie and the girls became puzzled when no flowers bloomed.

'Do you think they've had enough sun?' Mary asked when they were both in the garden one afternoon, peering at them. 'Or enough water?'

Annie furrowed her brow. 'Maybe they're not daffodils,' she concluded.

'What are you doing, Mum?' said an alarmed Mary, as her mother grabbed hold of the top of one stem and began to pull it out of the ground.

'Just looking,' she said, and what popped out of the soil had her whooping with laughter.

'It's a spring onion!' she declared.

'It's huge!' said Mary.

71

'Come on,' said a delighted Annie, 'help me pull them up.' One after another, they pulled the onions out of the ground, crying with laughter. 'At least we can eat these. You can't eat daffodils!'

It was the first time in what seemed like an age that Mary had heard her mother laughing so heartily, and she cherished the moment.

There was one thing about working at Baker's that Mary didn't like, and that was the unofficial job of smearing Eileen's legs with 'liquid stockings' from a bottle whenever she was going out and wanted to look her best. Wartime rationing had meant that the availability of stockings, along with other cosmetics, was sparse so women had to be inventive. Various tanning solutions in tins or bottles were on sale, which could be applied either by hand or with cotton wool. Once the solution had dried, it took a steady hand to draw a line up the back of the legs with an eyeliner pencil to represent the stocking seam. An even cheaper way of doing it was with tea or gravy but that could cause embarrassment if it rained and started to wash off.

Eileen didn't trust herself to make a good job of it so she would ask Mary to do it for her. Mary hated touching her legs but felt it would be too impolite to refuse. Anyway, it didn't happen often and Mary was generally upbeat, feeling happy at work and at home, where things were about to change . . .

'We're moving out,' Mary Eddicott said to Annie as she joined her downstairs in her kitchen. 'They've found us a bungalow, just off the High Street. There'll be more room for us and you'll have a lot more room here.'

Fitting In

'When will you be going?' Annie asked, feeling a mixture of relief that her family would have more space but also a sadness that she would be split from her old friend. They had stuck together since leaving Bermondsey and shared and supported each other throughout these extraordinary times.

'We should be gone by the end of the week,' Mary replied. Annie gave a little smile.

'Cheer up!' Mary laughed. 'We'll only be round the corner. It'll be better for us both.' Annie felt comforted by Mary's reaction and she reached out to her to share a warm embrace.

The Jarmans helped the Eddicotts to pack up some of their belongings and to settle into their new abode. The two families remained close and the children continued to see each other at school each day anyway.

Sheila, Kath and Pat had moved out of the emergency evacuee school in the village hall and had been assimilated into Hailsham County Junior School in Grovelands Road, a short walk away along the main road. They were still being taught by Miss Mobbs, and Sheila hated it there just as much as she had hated it at the village hall. She longed to be back at her old school in Dockhead, St Joseph's, and hadn't realized until now how fond she had been of it!

Joan, meanwhile, was still embarrassing herself at the secondary school in Battle Road. This time in a history lesson. She liked her history teacher, Miss Foster, mainly because her lessons seemed very informal yet informative, and there seldom seemed to be any essays to write.

'We never have to write anything, Mum,' she told Annie. 'She just sits there and talks to us, and we can ask questions and she tells us the answers. I really like her.'

73

The Sisters of Battle Road

The subject was Ancient Rome and, eager to shine as usual, Joan was first off the mark when Miss Foster asked the class if they knew the names of the Roman fighters who went into combat in the Colosseum.

Joan's hand shot up. She knew this one. Time to show just how bright she could be.

'Yes, Joan?' said the teacher.

'Gladioli, miss!' she answered. The class erupted into laughter and Joan went bright red once more.

Joan's penchant for a quick reply could also serve her well, however. The Jarman girls had very few clothes, just a day dress each, and the younger ones only had one pair of socks. This meant Annie was constantly washing and drying so that they had something clean to wear each day. As soon as their nightdresses were on, the day's dirty laundry went in the sink to soak, drying overnight near the open fire, and Annie seemed to be darning their garments constantly. The wartime slogan of 'make do and mend' had been something that Annie and her girls had been putting into practice all their lives.

One morning at school, a girl in Joan's class looked her up and down, and asked snootily, 'Is that the only dress you've got? You wear that every day.'

Mortified, yet thinking quickly, Joan lied, 'Oh no, this is just my school dress. I have other clothes for the weekends.'

The little money the family did have mostly went on food. As it became ever more scarce, and with rationing increasing, news of the arrival of a fresh lamb joint or decent sausages at the butcher's, tomatoes at the grocer's or a fresh batch of bread at the baker's would quickly be whispered from one friend to another and send them scurrying to the shops. Sometimes Annie would open her front door to see what the commotion was, and a familiar face would shout breathlessly, 'The butcher's! Sausages!'

It frequently resulted in queues forming outside shops, with women often joining the back of the line without even knowing what they were queuing for. But most of them didn't mind. It was a useful way to meet and gossip about what was happening locally as well as to have the occasional useful discussion about what was going on in the war. Many of the women had sons or husbands – sometimes both – fighting abroad.

After eight months of relatively little conflict, things were about to change dramatically.

'They've invaded Holland,' a local woman said to Annie one afternoon as she joined the queue outside the baker's. Annie felt a chill run through her. It was 10 May 1940 and the start of Hitler's plan to invade France and the Low Countries. The Nazis were suddenly moving at remarkable speed and the Allies were rattled. Throughout Britain people were buzzing with the rapidly unfolding news. On the same day as the Netherlands bore the imprint of the Nazi boot, in the House of Commons the Prime Minister Neville Chamberlain formally lost a vote of no confidence and was compelled to resign. He was immediately succeeded in office by the First Lord of the Admiralty, Winston Churchill.

On 13 May, German forces ploughed through the Ardennes in Belgium, crossing the Meuse River into France and crushing French resistance. Two days later, the Netherlands surrendered. Annie had listened to the shocking news on the wireless in her kitchen. 'And they said it would all be over by Christmas,' she said to Mary Eddicott, as they joined the queue at the baker's. They, like everyone else, felt more vulnerable now than ever at the thought of German soldiers just across the English Channel – the fear of invasion had never been higher.

The wireless became the most important source of escalating news as one dramatic event after another unfolded. On the evening of 14 May 1940, Annie and the older girls gathered around the wireless as the War Secretary, Anthony Eden, gave a broadcast announcing the creation of the Local Defence Volunteers, which later became known as the Home Guard. It called on men aged between seventeen and sixty-five, who were not in military service, to help defend their country against an invasion. Enrolment at police stations across the country was enthusiastic in the coming days and weeks.

Signposts and place names were removed throughout the country to confuse invading Germans and posters with slogans urging the populace not to enter into conversation with strangers – 'Be like dad, keep mum' and 'Careless talk costs lives' – were pasted up. In the South, the ringing of church bells was banned and they would only be sounded by the military or police if there was an invasion. Large concrete boulders were dotted across fields and long ditches dug to hinder enemy tanks should they make it across the Channel.

There was even more alarm when news came that the British Expeditionary Force, which had been sent to France to help their defence against invasion, found itself trapped along the northern coast of the country with the remains of the Belgian and French armies. An emergency evacuation from Dunkirk – known as Operation Dynamo – was put into place across the Channel, beginning on

27 May. An appeal for civilian vessels to come to the aid of stranded troops resulted in a flotilla of 900 naval and civilian craft crossing the Channel under RAF protection. By 4 June, a total of 338,226 soldiers had been brought back to Britain safely.

In a peculiarly British way, retreat was spun into victory in the minds of the majority of the people, fed by newspaper headlines such as 'Saved' and 'Disaster Turned to Triumph'. But even Churchill, that master of stirring oration, cautioned that 'Wars are not won by evacuations' and that 'What has happened in France and Belgium is a colossal military disaster.'

After France surrendered to the Germans on 22 June, Churchill gave the ominous warning, 'The Battle of France is over. I expect that the Battle of Britain is about to begin.'

In Hailsham, Annie listened to the wireless, wide-eyed in horror, and devoured any piece of information she could lay her hands on.

'What you reading, Mum?' Joan asked her mother one afternoon, as Annie sat in the kitchen engrossed in a leaflet.

Startled, Annie folded up the leaflet rapidly. 'Oh, nothing,' she said quickly, adjusting her expression to neutral. 'Nothing much of interest.'

But Annie was scared. Having been evacuated to so-called safety, Hailsham and other towns and coastal ports in the South of England were now recognized as being likely landing grounds for German parachutists, should an invasion occur. She had been reading a leaflet published by the Ministry of Defence that had been dropped through the letterbox that morning, entitled 'If the Invader Comes – what to do and how to do it'.

The opening paragraph had set her heart racing. 'The Germans threaten to invade Great Britain,' it read. 'If they do so they will be driven out by our Navy, our Army and our Air Force. Yet the ordinary men and women of the civilian population will also have their part to play.'

It went on to urge that unless ordered to evacuate, people should 'STAY PUT'. They were not to believe rumours or spread them, they should be suspicious of strangers and deny the enemy such things as food, transport and maps. Furthermore, they were urged to organize resistance at shops and factories, and to block roads with trees or cars in order to hinder the enemy advance if necessary.

Just a few weeks later, when Hitler turned his attention to London, Annie thanked her lucky stars that they were no longer in Bermondsey. During that long hot summer of 1940, the Luftwaffe started bombing her home town and other major cities in what became known as the Blitz – short for the German *Blitzkrieg*, meaning 'lightning war'. Annie feared for Pierce and her parents' safety, and the knot inside her stomach tightened every time an enemy plane flew over the South of England on its way to the capital. The children too, worried about their father and would pray for him every night before they fell asleep, each absorbed in their individual entreaties.

Sheila found it particularly hard to concentrate on lessons in the classroom whenever she heard the roar of engines in the sky, which seemed to reverberate inside the very bodies of those on the ground. She spent much of her time looking out of the window, worried sick that one of those planes was heading for London – for Abbey Street – to drop its load on their house and her father.

Fitting In

On one such day at school, she was startled out of her thoughts with a jump when Miss Mobbs shouted, 'Pay attention, Sheila Jarman!'

At home that evening, a tearful Sheila told Annie what had happened. 'I hate her, Mum. I hate school. She hates me. And I'm worried about Daddy.'

'Daddy will be safe. They're using the Underground to shelter during air raids,' Annie assured her, while not feeling particularly comforted by this herself.

As more and more German planes flew in, often blotting out the sun and casting foreboding shadows on the ground, the RAF met them in the skies in an aerial fight that became known as the Battle of Britain. Major British cities, including Birmingham, Liverpool, Glasgow, Manchester, Sheffield and Coventry, were all targeted and suffered extensive damage. To Annie, it felt as though nowhere was safe. Her job was to protect her children, but she knew that their wellbeing was out of her control.

At night, in their beds in Battle Road, the girls heard the familiar drone of enemy aircraft heading for London, along with the intermittent clacking of anti-aircraft guns in the distance, trying to bring them down, with the aid of searchlights, before they could get any further. In the midst of this fiery hell, Annie received a letter from Pierce. As soon as she began to read, her face became ashen and a sick feeling rose from the pit of her stomach.

'Abbey Street has been hit,' wrote Pierce. 'The house has been badly damaged. We can no longer live there. It's just a shell.'

He went on to say that, thankfully, Annie's parents – along with her brother Mike – had been sheltering safely in the cellar of the nearby Royal Oak pub when it happened.

Pierce, as usual, had been at his sisters' house. Even before the war, when the family had all been living together at home, Pierce was a frequent visitor to his sisters', much to Annie's irritation. Whenever she couldn't find him, she would comment, 'He'll be "down home" again', meaning at his sisters' house, his second home. This unusual expression was taken up by Annie's daughters and even Pierce's sisters were often themselves referred to as 'down home'. Now Annie thanked God that Pierce had been 'down home' when it most mattered.

Despite her great relief that her loved ones were safe, Annie was shocked by how easily the bomb might have resulted in their death. She was stunned that their family home, where they had brought up their children and where they had had so many memorable experiences, had been wiped out in a second.

Although she and Pierce didn't have many possessions, the house had contained some furniture she had put herself into debt to buy, paying off the amount in weekly instalments. There were also framed family photographs and other bits and bobs inside, which might not have seemed much to others but they were what made the house a home. Now, all gone, it brought the war close to her. It became personal in a way that it hadn't been before. Away from the children, she allowed herself a few tears – one of the rare occasions she gave in to her emotions during those years away from home.

The girls had most of their belongings with them in Hailsham but they too shared treasured memories of their life in Abbey Street, and were saddened at the thought of a German bomb destroying the family home. It made the future all the more uncertain.

Fitting In

'What will we do when we go back, Mum?' asked Sheila that evening, hands held apart in front of her, some wool looped around them, which Annie was using to knit a cardigan for young Anne.

'I don't know,' said Annie quietly, feeling vulnerable. 'But the most important thing is that we're all safe. Remember that in your prayers tonight and thank God for it.'

Pierce had told her in the letter that he had moved in with his sisters for the time being. 'They'll love that,' she thought to herself wryly. 'Having their beloved brother back.' Her own parents and brother Mike, meanwhile, were living in temporary accommodation until something more permanent could be arranged – just three more displaced Londoners with nowhere to go.

Annie was worried about them all, and kept thinking about her father's beloved sunflowers and elderberry tree in the yard – now destroyed. Then she had a thought that gave her considerable comfort. The departure of the Eddicotts had given both large families some much-needed 'breathing space', as the billeting officer had described it. Now that they had moved on, Annie could fit her parents and Mike in at Battle Road, if they were willing to move to the countryside. She was about to write back to Pierce with her idea when she realized that he would be visiting at the weekend, as usual, so she would see him before her letter could reach London.

That Friday, Pierce's arrival in Hailsham was greeted with extra-warm hugs from Annie and the girls, who quizzed him all about the bombing.

Later that evening, when Annie had told him her plan, Pierce asked, 'Are you sure you want to do that? You'll be crowded again. And it's pretty crowded already, especially when I'm here. And they're old now – they're both eighty-two. They might not want to come.'

'They're my family, Pierce. You have to take care of your own,' she said, without any thought of his sisters. 'Besides, I want them here. Away from London.' She paused. 'I want you here too. Can't you find a job?'

Pierce sighed. 'Not a proper one. I've got a decent job in London with decent pay. Besides, the Government is telling those who have jobs to carry on as normal. We can't all decamp to the countryside.' He smiled at Annie. 'As long as you and the girls are safe, I'll be fine.'

Despite knowing how much he missed his family, Annie suspected that he wouldn't have wanted to leave London anyway. Hailsham was very alien to him – less so now to her and the girls – and he would miss his friends, the sights and smells of the capital, the familiarity, the pubs. He had always enjoyed a pint. She too missed London and her old friends very much but it played on her mind constantly: Would London be destroyed by German bombers? Would there be anything left to return to?

The following Friday saw the return of Pierce, this time with Annie's parents and Mike. For the girls, this wasn't something that they welcomed. In their opinion, Tom and Kate lacked the warmth of most grandparents. Tom only ever wore a dark suit and a black homburg, and Kate dressed in her usual long black skirt, apron and black straw bonnet, always with a money bag tied around her waist. The darkness of their clothes seemed to reflect their manner.

That evening, the older girls helped Annie cook a meal of meat stew with carrots and boiled potatoes. It was a large family affair, with everyone gathered around the kitchen table as they had a lot of news and gossip to share. Annie wanted to hear about all the families left behind in Bermondsey, whose houses were still standing, and what had become of those who were now homeless. She also grilled her parents to find out what the men who were left behind without wives and children were getting up to in their absence – gently ribbing Pierce, who laughed at her thinly veiled attempt to discover how much time he was spending in the pub. Annie's parents assured her he was behaving himself.

For her part, Annie told her parents about life in Hailsham and how different they would find it from the hustle and bustle of London, while the girls chipped in with encouraging tidbits about how their grandparents would love the quiet and safety of the Sussex town. But as grateful as they were to be taken in, Tom and Kate were keen to return to Bermondsey, just as soon as the local council could find them somewhere else to live.

Annie, however, was so relieved at her mother and father's escape from the danger of bomb-ridden London, that she had not fully reckoned on the danger posed to her elderly parents by the house's precariously situated toilet at the top of the staircase. It was to prove more damaging to her mother than anything the Luftwaffe had ever thrown at her . . .

After they had eaten their meal, Kate excused herself to go to the lavatory.

'I'll come with you, Mum,' said Annie, concerned about the steep stairs and the dark hallway.

'I don't need anyone to take me to the toilet,' Kate replied a little brusquely. 'I'm not that decrepit . . . yet.'

'No, I know, it's just that the stairs are steep and the toilet is in an awkward position. We're all used to it now but it's a bit tricky.' Annie shadowed her mother as she made her way up the stairs slowly and into the lavatory.

'Give me a call, Mum, when you're coming down,' she said.

'I'm fine. Don't fuss,' Kate replied. As her mother closed the lavatory door, Annie walked back down the stairs and rejoined her family in the kitchen. She perched on her chair, keeping an ear tuned for the sound of the lavatory flushing so that she could assist her mother back down the stairs. Her concentration faded as she became more and more engrossed in the conversation, though. Suddenly, there came a loud thump, followed by the unmistakeable sound of a body tumbling down the stairs and yelps of pain. The children shot out of the room to investigate, followed quickly by Annie and Pierce.

'It's Grandma!' shouted Kath. 'She's fallen down the stairs!'

'Mum!' cried Annie, crouching down at Kate's side. But her mother didn't stir. Annie got to her feet. 'I'll fetch Rosie Goldsmith from next door. She's a nurse.' With that, she hurried out.

While Annie was gone, Kate started to come to her senses.

'Your ribs OK?' a concerned Pierce asked, watching her pat herself around the midriff. 'Is anything broken?'

'I was checking my money belt,' said Kate gravely. 'It seems to be intact.' The girls, much relieved, exchanged amused glances with each other. This was their grandmother through and through.

Despite having fallen from the top to the bottom of the

stairs, somehow Kate had suffered little more than a few bruises and a loss of dignity. Pierce helped her to her feet and into the living room where he made her comfortable in an armchair, as her husband showered her with an uncharacteristic public display of affection, placing his hand on her shoulder and asking, 'All right, old thing?'

Pierce went next door to find Annie and tell her that her mother wasn't too badly hurt after all, and that neither nurse nor ambulance was required. Annie, who had feared the worst, couldn't quite believe the remarkably good shape her mother was in.

'Mum,' she said anxiously, as she entered the living room. 'I *told* you . . . Are you OK?'

Kate frowned and replied crossly, 'What a ridiculous place to put a toilet!'

The Battle of Britain was escalating with swarms of German planes flying over the South of England, many of which passed over Hailsham and caused the girls to become increasingly worried about their father in London. Even their own safe haven began to feel ever more vulnerable as the Luftwaffe targeted British defences on the south coast. In addition, German pilots would jettison unused bombs on their way back home, to ensure their planes were light enough not to run out of fuel.

On 17 July 1940, war came closer to Hailsham than ever before. Twelve Spitfires of 64 Squadron were patrolling Beachy Head, close to Eastbourne, when they were met by German Messerschmitt 109s. One of the Spitfires was hit and, in the early afternoon, the plane crashed on open ground at Hempstead Lane, just over a mile from Battle Road. The young pilot, Donald Taylor, was admitted to

Eastbourne Hospital with wounds including fragments of metal embedded in his head, torso, right arm and right leg. Thankfully, his injuries weren't life threatening and he returned to flying a couple of months later in September.

News of the plane crash spread through the schoolrooms and over the garden fences in no time. The majority of the children chatted excitedly about the pilot's lucky escape, marvelling at the courage of the RAF fighters.

'He must be *so* brave,' said one of the boys in Kath's class. 'When I'm older I want to be a pilot, just like him.'

To help take her mind off the war, Joan, who had always been a voracious reader, found solace in the escapism that novels brought. Back home in Bermondsey, she used to take four or five books at a time out of the large and comprehensive library in Spa Road, and she was delighted to find that Hailsham also had a library, albeit a smaller one, where she could continue this practice.

She had thoroughly enjoyed *Little Women* by Louisa May Alcott, which told the story of sisters Meg, Jo, Beth and Amy March, growing up with their mother during the American Civil War while their father was away with the Union troops, acting as chaplain. The March sisters might have been living through a war in the same way as the Jarman girls were but Joan thought the American Civil War seemed a much more romantic backdrop than Hitler and his scary Nazi soldiers.

Joan went on to devour the sequels *Good Wives*, *Little Men* and *Jo's Boys*. After that she was charmed, like so many other children around the world, by the adventures of eleven-year-old orphan Anne Shirley of Nova Scotia in *Anne of Green Gables*. There were even more sequels to this novel than *Little Women* and Joan had delightful times reading them all, anywhere she could find a small place in the house offering the relative peace to do so. Away from her other sisters for a while, she immersed herself in a different world. Whenever Annie couldn't find Joan, she knew that she would eventually track her down to the quietest corner of the house where she would discover her with her nose in a book.

Although Joan was never going to be top of the class at school, she did push herself and reading was her first love. She enjoyed English immensely, and when it came to compositions she would write avidly, page after page, not quite knowing when to stop. She was also good at Art and other practical lessons, such as the housewifery class they had every week.

Just as Mary had done in London, all the sisters learnt how to do housework at school – laundering, ironing and even scrubbing floors. The Jarman girls were quite used to this type of thing already because Annie had always given them chores to do around the house. Whenever Joan had to take in items to work on in class – a sheet, pillowcase or towel to wash, dry and iron – Annie was delighted, considering it one less chore she had to worry about at home.

At school in Bermondsey, Joan had also learnt needlework but the dressmaking class at Hailsham Senior Mixed School – like all the lessons there – was more advanced than she had been used to.

'They have a sewing machine, Mum,' she told Annie.

'That's very grand,' Annie replied. 'I could do with one of those at home.'

While the local Hailsham pupils had become used to working on the machine, it was all new to Joan. At home, the Jarman girls sewed by hand under the tutelage of Annie and they enjoyed doing it. They could ask Annie how to do this or that and she would patiently show them, but at school Joan felt too embarrassed to keep asking her teacher questions in front of the other pupils. She was so far behind and there was yet another humiliating moment for her during a lesson, when the teacher told the class that they could make something of their own choosing.

Joan decided that she would like to make a dress for her sister Anne, who was now one year old, but things went wrong from the start. They had to cut out the material as their teacher walked around the classroom, watching to see how they were getting on. Pleased with what she had done, Joan laid down two pieces of cut material which would form the basis of the dress. One of the other girls had noticed her mistake, though, and couldn't wait to bring it to the teacher's attention.

'Miss! Miss!' she called out. 'She's cut two left sides!'

Once more Joan felt her face flushing. The teacher told Joan calmly to have another go but she was upset for the rest of the day at how some of her classmates couldn't wait to laugh at her.

Back at home that evening, Mary sensed that Joan, who was being unusually quiet, was unhappy.

'Is something the matter, Joan?' she asked, when they were both in the kitchen preparing the evening meal.

'Oh, it's nothing. Just school. You're lucky you don't have to go any more.'

'Going to work isn't a barrel of fun either,' Mary pointed out.

'I didn't mind school back home.'

'Yes, you did.'

Well, perhaps she hadn't always loved school. But this was different.

'Whenever I do something wrong the other kids laugh at me,' said Joan after a while. 'Like today, when I was making a dress for Anne and cut out two left sides.'

Mary stopped what she was doing for a moment and turned to face her sister.

'You've got to make out that you're not bothered. If it had been me, I'd have laughed along with them.'

'But I'm not like you. You think *everything* is a laugh.'

'Not everything,' Mary reasoned. 'I didn't think my job at Greens was funny. But if you get upset every time something goes wrong, then the girls are more likely to carry on teasing.'

It was sensible advice. Joan nodded and gave her sister a small smile, resolving there and then not to take it to heart every time something didn't go as she'd have liked.

School life did improve as she determined to get on and make the best of things, but nonetheless, at the end of term Joan could scarcely believe it when she was awarded third prize for her efforts across all subjects. This time her face glowed with pride as head teacher Mr Russell handed her a brand-new atlas in front of her applauding peers.

After school finished that day, Joan, brimming with pride, rushed home and burst into the kitchen, calling breathlessly, 'Mum! Mum! Look what I've got!'

'What is it?' asked a smiling Annie, drying her hands on her apron.

A beaming Joan showed her the book. 'It was my prize at school. For third place.'

'That's wonderful, Joan,' said Annie. 'Third place!

Amongst all those children! I knew you'd do well if you stuck at it. You're as good as anyone. Just remember that.'

Joan treasured the book, carefully handling the pages so as not to damage them, as though they were part of an important historical document. From then on, she felt much more confident and far happier at school, her prize testament to the fact that she was at least as smart as those around her.

To the girls' relief, Kate, Tom and Mike only stayed at Battle Road for a few nights before they found rooms for rent in a house further along the road. The girls had been delighted when their grandparents had brought their wind-up gramophone and record collection to the house but were even more pleased when Tom and Kate left them behind after moving out. It meant that the girls could play the records whenever they liked – so long as Annie agreed. Then again, Annie had always liked music and singing, so she rarely objected.

There was quite a lot of classical musical, which Tom enjoyed, and songs from the Italian operatic singer Enrico Caruso. In stark contrast, they also found rousing cockney songs from the long-running music-hall show *Casey's Court*. This featured comedian Will Murray and a cast of child performers – including a young Charlie Chaplin – who acted as cheeky cockney street urchins in a variety of sketches and songs. The show, which ran from the early 1900s to the 1950s, was so popular that the phrase 'It's like Casey's Court in here!' became used whenever there was an unruly gathering of children, and the girls often heard it directed at them by Annie.

Casey's Court records featured cheeky remarks and

songs such as 'Jolly Good Company', 'Whistling In The Dark', 'It Always Starts To Rain' and 'Tie A Little String Around Your Finger', all accompanied by a barrel organ, somebody playing the spoons and other ad hoc instruments. The Jarman sisters loved listening to these records because they made them laugh and smile, and they soon got to know all of the words, which they would sing merrily around the house. Annie would often join in and although they made her smile too, a small part of her felt that they were rather common. She hoped the neighbours couldn't hear them.

There were other family visitors to Battle Road over the summer. Most weekends, Pierce's sisters would accompany him, much to the annoyance of Annie and her girls. The girls' cousin Kit stayed with them for a while too. It was Kit who, knowing that Mary was seeking a full-time job, noticed an advert in the window of the newsagent's in the High Street. An office worker was needed at the Silverlight Laundry in North Street.

'An office worker,' said Annie, smiling at Mary when she told her about it. 'That sounds impressive, Mary. You should definitely go for that.'

'But it's not anything I've done before, Mum,' replied Mary. 'Do you think I'll be able to do it?'

'I'm sure you can,' said Annie. It was the same positive message she gave to all her daughters. 'You'll learn.'

The laundry was owned by Mr and Mrs Gates, a couple originally from London. When Mary went along to apply for the job, Mrs Gates liked the fact that she was a fellow Londoner, confiding in her, 'I like having girls from London working for me. They've got more sense than the locals.'

'I got it, Mum!' Mary told Annie excitedly when she

returned home that day, beaming from ear to ear. 'I start tomorrow.'

Annie too was delighted at the thought of having an office worker as a daughter. It was definitely a step in the right direction and she managed to drop it casually into many conversations with the other mums. This was something she didn't mind the neighbours hearing.

However, it quickly became apparent, both to Mary and to Mrs Gates, that Mary wasn't cut out for office work. She had to help with the accounts, and dealing with figures was not her forte. Mrs Gates, despite insisting that her staff address her as 'madam', was a kind and caring woman, and she took pity on Mary, offering her a job in the sorting and packing department instead. It was overseen by Mr Lavender, whose penchant for chewing tobacco made his breath smell considerably less sweet than his name.

Mary was grateful not to be sacked but found the work and conditions of her new role unpleasant. The main laundry floor had a staff of around thirty girls – some would be ironing, others packing. Mary had what she considered to be the worst job: sorting dirty washing and putting it into the large washing machines. However, as always, she could see the funny side of most situations and the rather unpleasant job was punctuated liberally with laughs.

The pockets of garments all had to be checked to make sure that they were empty before the clothes were put into the wash. Sylvia Blundell, who was working alongside Mary, was going through the pockets of several waiters' jackets that had come in from a local hotel, when she found what she thought was a long balloon. Deciding to have some fun, she blew it up and walked through the factory, playfully hitting the other girls on the head with it. As everyone screamed with laughter, Mrs Gates walked over to see what was causing so much hilarity.

'Sylvia, put that . . . *thing* away!' she cried, alarmed at the sight. It was only later that the girls learnt, from one of the older employees, that what they thought was a balloon had actually been a condom.

That summer, Mary and Joan's heads were being turned by the presence of overseas soldiers camped in the fields and woods off Battle Road. While most British soldiers were fighting abroad, the UK's defences along the south coast were shored up by thousands of Canadian troops. With their accents, uniforms and a certain swagger, they attracted many admiring looks from the local women and impressionable teenagers such as Mary and Joan.

During the day, these exciting young men were on manoeuvres and carrying out military exercises. At night, they would sit around the campfire, enjoying treats such as toasted cheese sandwiches. On Sundays, they would march smartly down the High Street to the parish church in the town centre, coinciding with the arrival of impressionable teenage girls. Church had never been so much fun.

By chance, Mary became a regular visitor to the Canadian troops' camp when she changed roles again at the Silverlight Laundry. She had been asked if she would like to move out of the sorting and packing department to become an assistant to the woman who drove one of the collection vans, picking up dirty washing from clients and returning it cleaned and pressed.

'Yes, please,' she had told Mrs Gates eagerly, keen to get away from the stifling heat and chemical smell of the laundry.

Mary enjoyed her new role with the driver, Mrs Westcomb, although she did miss working with the other girls she'd befriended in the sorting department. However, after a few months, Mrs Westcomb left the company to be with her husband, and an eighteen-year-old local lad named Gordon Mitchell applied for her job and got it. As he was waiting to be called up for the army, the laundry manager, Mr Leslie, told him to teach Mary how to drive so that she would be able to take over once he had gone. Mary found it quite easy to learn, as there was so little traffic on the country roads – petrol was rationed and anyone who owned a car was careful not to use too much fuel.

When Gordon's call-up papers duly arrived, Mary took the driving seat and thoroughly enjoyed it. To her delight, she found that she got on really well with the girl of her own age assigned to be her assistant, Iris Packham. The working day became huge fun and the pair became good friends outside of work too.

One of the stops on their laundry round was the Canadian soldiers' camp. With her slim figure and flaming-red hair, Mary attracted quite a bit of attention from the troops, including one young man in particular, whose appearance startled her. He was an Aboriginal Canadian who lived on a reservation back home. Known as Woppamoose, he was a hulking, taciturn man, and the younger Jarman girls were frightened of him whenever they spotted him in town. They had never seen anyone like him, so Mary was surprised and a little unnerved when one day he asked her to go to the pictures with him. Not quite knowing what to say, she eventually settled on, 'I'll have to let you know.' Back home, when she talked to her mother about it, Annie was adamant.

'No,' she said. 'You don't know him.'

Fitting In

However, to both Mary and Annie's surprise, Pierce took umbrage.

'He's a fella in a foreign country, fighting for Britain,' he said. 'You go to the pictures with him, Mary.'

Mary could hardly believe that her father, usually very protective of his daughters, was encouraging her to go on a date. Annie, despite her rather domineering personality, thought better of arguing with her husband when he was in such spirits. Mary hadn't been keen on going out with Woppamoose but now felt that she had to, so she decided on some back-up.

'You come, too,' she said to Joan. But Joan had no intention of playing gooseberry.

'I can't come with you. He's taking *you* out,' she replied. 'He won't want *me* there.'

'Well, just come and sit nearby . . . Please.'

Joan considered this. 'I'm not sitting on my own but I'll ask Maureen if she wants to come,' she said.

At the cinema, they sat through a typically jingoistic Pathé News reel putting the best gloss, as always, on the latest confrontation on the war front. This time, it was dramatic footage of Germans shelling British merchant ships in the Channel from large guns on the French coast, complete with noisy explosions. As the packed audience sat spellbound in the darkness, a cheer went up when the narrator said, 'But the fact remains that not a single ship is hit or lost.'

There was a further cheer when he added, 'The Hun are not having it all their own way. Earlier in the bombardment, RAF take to the air, swiftly crossing the Channel and searching out the gun emplacement.' In this way they were able to 'blast the enemy into silence'.

The audience then relaxed to watch Errol Flynn star in *Virginia City* as a Union officer who escapes from a Confederate prison and discovers that the former commander of the prison – played by Randolph Scott – is planning to send $5 million in gold to save the Confederacy.

That evening at the cinema, Joan and her best friend Maureen turned out to have one of the most entertaining nights of their lives. Not that they watched much of the film – despite the allure of the dashing Errol Flynn. Seated just behind Mary and Woppamoose, the pair of them giggled throughout at the sight of his huge frame next to seven-and-a-half-stone Mary. They were an absurd-looking couple.

Once home, Annie joined in the laughter when Joan told her all about it, and Mary couldn't help but smile too. Annie's laughter brought on a severe coughing fit, though, and the girls looked at one another in concern. She hadn't been well for the past couple of days, and they were worried.

It wasn't an entirely new problem. Back in London they were used to her taking to her bed after a severe bout of rasping that would have her doubled over in pain and gasping for breath. She would have chest pains and night-time fever, and feel exhausted. On several occasions she had spent time in hospital to recuperate, where the 'treatment' was little more than plenty of rest, regular fresh air on the veranda or anywhere else outside, and healthy food. The fresh air of the Hailsham countryside had been keeping the cough at bay for the most part but now it had come back with a vengeance.

'Are you OK, Mum?' Mary asked. It was a while before Annie had the breath and energy to answer.

Fitting In

'I just need to rest for a while,' she said, hating to make a fuss.

Over the next few days, as the coughing fits and wheezing increased in regularity and severity, Annie grew worried too. The illness which she had done her best not to think about was becoming worse.

CHAPTER 4

The Telegram

Happier times. Annie pushing Mary and Joan in a pram, with Pierce (right) and Annie's brother, Uncle Mike (left).

THE GIRLS HAD become used to their mother's ill health in London but were blissfully unaware of just what was wrong with her – and Annie considered them too young to know. Both she and a worried Pierce never directly addressed their greatest fear of what it might be. Besides, as a proud Londoner, Annie – just like her mother – didn't want to make a fuss. She didn't want her girls to worry.

Sometimes she could be very poorly indeed, with a dry, hacking cough. At its most violent, it would leave her on her knees, red-faced, weak and wheezing, but after a day or two of rest – sometimes taking to her bed – she would get better and be able to carry on as before. At least until the next time.

In spite of her illness, Annie prided herself on keeping a spotless house in Bermondsey, and the children frequently saw her on her hands and knees, scrubbing the floor until it shone, when they came in from playing in the street. She had standards to meet after all. Ill or not.

'Wipe your feet! Take your shoes off!' she would shout, before resuming the song she'd been singing as she cleaned. The soap suds all around her might have inspired her particular favourite, 'I'm Forever Blowing Bubbles'.

One afternoon, she was singing at the top of her voice while scrubbing the hallway floor when she started coughing so violently that she struggled to breathe.

'Are you all right, Mummy?' a concerned Sheila asked, emerging from the living room to find her mother on all fours, her chest heaving and face covered in a sheen of sweat.

'Yes. Just need . . . sit down,' Annie managed to wheeze. Sheila helped her to her feet and to an armchair. Annie collapsed into it heavily and, after several minutes, eventually caught her breath. Just a little while later, Sheila marvelled as her mother got back to scrubbing the floor. It was not Annie's amazing powers of recovery that most impressed the seven-year-old girl, but how she was able to pick up the song lyrics exactly where she left off!

'It's just a cough,' Annie would say airily. 'It doesn't last.'

Pierce appeared to be happy to believe her – Annie considered herself to be too busy being a mother to let illness get in the way.

In the spring of 1937, Pierce finally persuaded Annie to see the doctor. After much questioning, she admitted that she had been coughing up blood and, when things were that bad, she often felt feverish too. Having examined her, the doctor told her in grave tones that she had contracted tuberculosis, and that she needed to go to hospital for closer examination.

Tuberculosis – often nicknamed 'consumption' because the illness's gradual emaciation of the body meant that those afflicted seemed to be consumed – was a highly infectious disease, easily spread, and, in cramped urban areas such as Bermondsey, was much feared as a result.

With no cure at that time, a combination of rest, fresh air and a decent diet in hospitals or sanatoriums achieved a modicum of success, not least because it formed a healthier lifestyle, and also kept the patients away from others who might contract the disease from them. However, the prognosis for those with tuberculosis was often poor.

'I can't go into hospital,' Annie had said to her doctor, with rising fear. 'I have a family to bring up. It's impossible.'

The doctor had been firm: she needed to go.

Back at home she remained defiant but Pierce, too, could be stubborn at times. Like Annie, he had secretly feared the possibility of this diagnosis. Now he was adamant that if a spell in hospital would be of benefit to her, then she must go. He promised that the girls would be fine and that Annie's parents could help out whilst she was away.

Eventually Annie had relented, and she and Pierce travelled by bus to St Olave's Hospital in nearby Rotherhithe. A huge Victorian building built in the 1870s, the hospital sat behind imposing iron gates between two identical houses, which were also owned by the hospital trust. The male and female wings of the building were separated by the administrative block, and the whole hospital was nestled on two acres of land, backing on to Southwark Park. It wasn't quite the clean, cold mountain air of Switzerland, but it gave Annie the chance to take it easy for a while.

To no one in the family's surprise, Annie hated it there and hated being away from her family. Mary accompanied her father to visit Annie on a couple of occasions but it was felt best not to bring the younger girls. It wasn't practical to keep a mother isolated from her children at home but at least while she was recuperating in hospital the girls should stay away and not risk infection.

Annie remained at St Olave's for a little over a week before returning home, but it was not to be her last stay there. For the girls, their mother's frequent spells in hospital during this time in their lives instilled in them an independence and a practical attitude. They became adept at getting on with the domestic routine and by the age of eleven, Joan often found herself in the role of surrogate mother. She enjoyed cooking and, while their mother was in hospital, took a mature approach to ensuring that her sisters, as well as her father, had a meal every evening.

One morning, on her way to school, Joan was wondering what to do for tea that evening, when she thought how lovely it would be if they could have bread pudding – one of their favourites – just like their mum made it. The problem was, she had no idea what Annie's recipe was. So when she returned home she went straight downstairs to her grandmother to ask her how to make it. Kate told her what she would need and how to mix it, and to put it into a roasting tin before baking it in the oven for fifty minutes or so, until golden brown. Joan followed the instructions to the letter, and it proved to be such a success that Gran's recipe became part of Joan's cooking repertoire for the rest of her life.

That summer, during another of Annie's stints at St Olave's, Pierce went to visit her while the girls' grandparents took them to play in nearby Southwark Park. In the midst of a game, Sheila noticed something. She suddenly stopped and pointed towards the hospital. 'Look! It's Mum!'

Weak and frail, Annie had walked out onto the veranda and was waving down at them, smiling. The girls smiled and waved back energetically but each of them felt sadness at the sight of the forlorn and slight figure in the distance. She seemed very far removed from the cheerful, robust woman whose singing would resound throughout the house.

The seriousness of Annie's condition was brought home unexpectedly to Mary at school one day. Mary, then thirteen, had moved into the top class for her final year. All the teachers were nuns and she loved her form tutor, Sister Theresa, who had a nice way of treating her pupils – more like grown-ups, Mary thought, than children. Sister Theresa would tell them funny little stories but Mary was sometimes a bit slow in getting the joke and so there was often a delay before she started laughing. Once she got it, though, she couldn't stop giggling, so sometimes Sister Theresa would have to send her out of the classroom for a while to compose herself. On one such occasion, Mary was spotted in the hallway by the formidable headmistress, Sister Fidelis.

Mary was given advance warning that the sister was making her way along the corridor by the rattling of the large wooden rosary the nun wore around her waist. This always gave pupils time either to stop misbehaving or to make a prompt getaway. Mary had to think fast. Should she go back into the classroom after only a minute outside? No. Without further ado she scurried quietly to the nearby cloakroom and hid behind a rack of coats. However, Sister Fidelis' finely tuned ears must have detected a sound and, to Mary's horror, she entered the cloakroom. With a thumping heart, Mary ducked lower.

'Who's there?' called the voice sternly. Trapped, Mary took a deep breath and revealed herself slowly.

'Mary Jarman! What on earth do you think you are doing?'

A sheepish Mary did her best to explain about having

to compose herself after giggling too much in class. Sister Fidelis looked down at her without comment for a few moments and Mary was terrified that she was going to have to endure one of the nun's favourite forms of punishment – making her pupils kneel on coconut matting whilst praying the rosary. It was an excruciatingly painful ordeal which left children with red and sore knees. This time, Sister Fidelis took a different tack and Mary was taken aback by her words.

'Your mother is seriously ill with tuberculosis,' Sister Fidelis said. 'You should be praying for her, not misbehaving. Now get yourself back to class and stop acting the fool!'

Mary felt sick to the stomach. She knew her mother had been in hospital but didn't know that tuberculosis was anything that required prayer. It took all of her willpower not to burst into tears as she slowly made her way back to class. Giggling was now the last thing on her mind.

Annie's willpower was even stronger, though, and saw her recover enough to leave hospital and return home to carry on with her life, much as she had always done. For the girls, thoughts of their mother's frailty receded for the time being.

Forever striving for better things for her family, and keen to rent a bigger home to accommodate her growing children, Annie was a frequent visitor to the local council. She wanted to move out of Bermondsey, which she didn't think was good enough for her. She wasn't going to accept just any alternative, though. She wanted a prettier, more spacious environment.

'There's a place going in Downtown,' the housing officer suggested, referring to an eastern region of Rotherhithe.

'I'm not going there!' Annie replied forcefully. 'That's worse than Bermondsey.'

'But you'll have more room,' the housing officer persisted.

'What about Grove Park?' said Annie, cutting him short. The southeast London suburb of Grove Park, near Lewisham, where Annie occasionally shopped, struck a chord with her aspirational nature. There, much of the farmland had been sold in the early 1930s and airy new villas had been built.

The housing officer shook his head. The exchange was a familiar showdown between him and Annie over the years – only brought to an end by wartime evacuation.

'I'll be back next week to see what you've got,' she said as she got up to leave.

In a sad twist of fate, Annie did get to reside in Grove Park. But it certainly wasn't the type of home she wanted.

With its imposing red-brick facade, grey slate roof, abundant chimney stacks and domed gatehouses on either side of its entrance, the magnificent Victorian building in the leafy London suburb might have been a grand stately home. However, the history of Grove Park Hospital always sent a shudder through those who had reason to stay there.

The ten-acre site had originally been built in 1902 as a workhouse for the poor, elderly and ill of Greenwich borough. The more able-bodied paid for their residence with the monotonous daily chore of breaking up granite, which was later sold to councils for road construction. Following the outbreak of the First World War in 1914 it was requisitioned by the Mechanical Transport Depot Service Corps. The residents were relocated to other workhouses while the grounds and buildings were used as a training and mobilization camp.

Then, in 1919, the workhouse was sold to the Metropolitan Asylums Board, who turned it into a hospital for the sick of South London. Grove Park Hospital specialized in the treatment of tuberculosis and so the building's grim reputation continued for successive generations. It had 299 beds – 117 for men along the north side of the main, three-storey building and 182 for women along the south.

After a particularly bad coughing attack, Annie was referred to Grove Park in the autumn of 1937 – her second hospital stay that year. As a specialist hospital, there was more attention to diet, rest and exercise for the patients than at St Olave's but, with no cure for tuberculosis, there was little more to be offered. A surgical option was sometimes carried out, called the pneumothorax (or plombage) technique, in which an infected lung was collapsed to reduce its volume and thus rest it, but this procedure had little proven benefit and its practice was mostly discontinued after 1946. It would not be until after the Second World War that a drug called streptomycin was developed, which proved to be extremely effective against TB. It paved the way for a rapid succession of anti-TB drugs in the following years. However, unfortunately for Annie, that was all in the future.

Annie acutely felt the irony of finally living in the area to which she aspired. It seemed like God was playing a joke on her – a joke in rather poor taste. In Grove Park, she felt increasingly miserable amongst the sick and dying, and yearned to be back home with her family, neighbours and friends, sharing a laugh, gossip or simply being fit and well enough to do household chores – whilst singing, of course. There was no singing here. Only the sounds of coughing, wheezing and moaning.

One day she had had a visit from a solemn doctor, who told her that her sickness wasn't going to go away and that, whilst they could make her comfortable, her long-term prognosis was not good.

'Well, I don't want to be here long term,' she told him.

'What I mean, Mrs Jarman, is that you will need to come to terms with the fact that the illness will reduce your life expectancy significantly.'

Annie stared at him, as it slowly dawned on her what he was really saying.

'How long?' she asked.

He told her that she probably had around ten months left to live.

Annie was too stunned to cry. That would come later, in private. Instead, once she had gathered her thoughts, her next reaction was a typically practical one.

'That's all the more reason to be with my family, then,' she said firmly. 'There's no point in spending the rest of my life *here*. I want to spend what's left of it back home.' She paused. 'Anyhow, I'm feeling a lot better. And they need me.'

Annie wasted no time in getting out of bed and into her clothes. She packed her belongings and a young porter, who she thought could only have been fourteen or fifteen, carried her suitcase down the stairs and outside. Annie thanked him before picking up the case to make the short walk to the bus stop. He smiled at her and, with the clumsy tactlessness of youth, remarked, 'I didn't think anyone ever walked out of this hospital.'

Annie had been so eager to flee the oppressive

surrounds of the hospital, there had been no time to tell anyone that she was coming home. None of her family knew that she had discharged herself. The girls were playing in the local park in Tooley Street when one of their friends arrived and told them that their mother was home. They ran back to Abbey Street, with spirits soaring, and charged into the house, where they found her standing in the kitchen. Annie cuddled them warmly. She had missed them all so much. The house might be crowded, the girls a little noisy, but it was home. It was life.

Pierce was startled when he returned home from work.

'My place is here, with you and the children,' she said before Pierce kissed her.

Annie explained that she had discharged herself and told her husband what the doctor had said. Pierce hugged her tightly and she felt a tear roll down her face.

After a few moments she released herself, wiped her face swiftly with her sleeve and said, 'Anyway. What do they know? They don't know me. I'll prove them wrong. And we'll keep it from the girls.'

She gave Pierce a quick peck on the cheek and walked off, leaving him to marvel at her bravery and resilience. And to hope to God that she was right.

In September 1940, Sheila left Hailsham Junior School in Grovelands Road to attend senior school in Battle Road. Although she was delighted to be away from Miss Mobbs, she was apprehensive about joining 'big school' and soon made up her mind that she hated this new one as much as she had hated her junior school.

Sheila hadn't really made any close friends amongst the local children, preferring to stick with the evacuees she knew from back in Bermondsey. At Hailsham Senior Mixed School, though, the only other evacuee in her year was her good friend Mary Eddicott – who shared the name with her mother – and she was convinced that the teachers didn't like either of them. Sheila particularly disliked the head teacher, Mr Russell, who was stern and made her quake with fear. Sometimes, when she saw him approaching in the corridor, she felt as though she was going to faint.

Despite all this, she did well in class, and each time it came to grading, she would find herself in the A section, even though she was convinced that she would be marked down each year.

Like Joan, Sheila was a voracious reader and was particularly good at English. However, it was PE that gave her the greatest pleasure. She was a good runner and won most of the races at the school's annual sports day, held at the rec. With the help of these small mercies, Sheila found herself settling in, and began to find school in Hailsham tolerable, if not enjoyable.

When not at school, Joan was becoming more of a homemaker. As Annie's illness became worse, she spent more and more time in bed recovering, or sitting in the armchair, too weak to do the chores. Despite her advanced years, Annie's mother also helped out and the younger girls did their bit with cooking, darning, cleaning and shopping. Everyone pitched in looking after baby Anne.

Occasionally, when need be, Annie recovered enough to show her fiery spirit, such as the afternoon she sent Joan into town to buy some potatoes. When Joan brought them home, Annie inspected them and turned up her nose at the fact that some of them were sprouting.

'You can't let them get away with that, Joan,' she said.

'These are much too old. We haven't got money to burn and it's not to be wasted on rubbish like this.' She leapt out of her armchair and put her coat on. 'Come on.'

'Where are we going?' Joan asked.

'Back to the shop. I'm going to give them a piece of my mind.'

Joan was not looking forward to the embarrassing episode this was likely to be, but she knew by now that it was pointless trying to stop her mother when she had set her mind to something. In the event, it was even more mortifying than Joan had anticipated. Annie stormed into the shop and emptied the contents of the bag over the counter, sending the potatoes rolling all over the floor.

The greengrocer looked petrified as Annie shouted, 'We might have come from London but we don't eat shit!'

He mumbled an apology and promptly gave Annie fresh potatoes. From then on, he made sure that the Jarmans were never given inferior produce.

Money was tight, as always, and Annie was adept at making a little go a long way. However, she also suffered the occasional lapse when her desire for something non-essential but nice took precedence, like the ill-fated piano she had bought in Bermondsey.

A warm, late summer's day inspired Annie and Mary Eddicott to catch the bus into Eastbourne for what was intended to be window shopping. They particularly liked looking at the nice things in the department stores and, in one of them, Annie saw a mantle clock in an oak case on one of the shelves. She was thinking how elegant it looked, with its silver face perched above twin decorative wooden mouldings, when a shop assistant approached and asked if she might be of help.

'I'm just looking, thank you,' said Annie. 'It's got a lovely deep tick-tock,' she added.

'That's not all,' said the lady, who then opened the glass case and moved the hand forward to three o'clock. There was a brief mechanical sound and then a beautiful chime as it struck the hour three times.

'Oh, that's lovely,' said a delighted Annie. 'Isn't that nice, Mary?'

The assistant smiled. 'I think it has the best chime of all the clocks here,' she said. 'Simple but quite loud and melodic for its size.'

Annie agreed.

'It's what they call Napoleon style – in the shape of his hat, see?' said the assistant, sensing a sale.

'Lovely,' said Annie again, and looked at Mary, who raised her eyebrows. 'We could do with one of these at home. It's good quality. And a lovely chimer.' She smiled at the assistant. 'I'll need to think about it,' she said, and they left the store.

Back home, Annie kept staring at the mantelpiece in the living room, thinking how nice the clock would look there. The more she looked, the more she thought how perfectly it would fit. Two days later, she went back to the store on her own and brought the clock home with her.

Pierce disapproved but tried not to show it, knowing how ill Annie was and how happy the purchase had made her.

'Just listen to that chime, Pierce.' She smiled, like a little girl with a birthday present. 'Sounds very regal, doesn't it? And it's good quality. I'm sure it will last for years and years.'

As Annie was making the house in Battle Road more

and more like a home, a couple of aerial incidents in quick succession made her wonder whether their new abode was doomed to suffer the same fate as 103 Abbey Street and whether, once again, they would lose all they possessed.

On the morning of 27 September, many Hailsham residents were witness to a spectacular aerial dog fight at low level in the skies. In recent days, the Luftwaffe had had several successes when German bombers, escorted by twin-engine Messerschmitt fighter planes, successfully hit the Bristol Aeroplane Company at Filton, causing extensive damage and killing over one hundred people. Around the same time, two raids in Woolston, Southampton, flattened the Supermarine factory, which manufactured Spitfires, with another hundred casualties.

The RAF was better prepared for the next attack, though, and as a formation of Junker 88s flew over the south coast, accompanied by protective Messerschmitt 100s, a stream of Hurricanes met them. As bullets flew and evasive action was taken, the German aircraft beat a hasty retreat back towards the Channel. However, a young RAF pilot named Percy Burton chased a Messerschmitt 110 towards Hailsham air space.

Just north of the town, Burton stopped firing, most likely because he was out of ammunition, and the two aircraft flew low over houses and treetops. Locals watched in amazement as the Hurricane then appeared to shunt the Messerschmitt from the rear and the tail unit of the 110 detached and dropped into a field, followed shortly by the rest of the aircraft. Unfortunately, the wingtip of Burton's plane had also been ripped off and he crashed into a large oak tree on New Barn Farm. Both pilots died.

The following month saw an RAF pilot run out of

fuel in his Spitfire after engaging in combat with some Messerschmitt 109s, and crash land at Pattenden's Farm in Battle Road. Pierce was having a drink at The Terminus pub in Station Road at the time of the crash, participating in a leisurely game of shove ha'penny. He was just lining up a coin at the edge of the board when one of the regular customers rushed in and said excitedly, 'A plane's come down in town! Right on Battle Road!'

A feeling of panic washed over Pierce as he feared for his family's safety. Without a second thought, he rushed outside, grabbed a bicycle leaning against the pub wall, and rode it home as fast as he could pedal. Bursting through the door, he shouted, 'Is everyone all right? Where's the plane?'

His daughters joined him in the kitchen. 'It came down on Pattenden's Farm, Dad,' said a wide-eyed Joan. 'We're all safe, don't worry,' she added.

'Where's Mummy?'

'Upstairs, resting.'

Breathing heavily after his panic-stricken dash, Pierce slumped into a chair with relief. 'I heard at The Terminus and cycled home as fast as I could,' he said. The girls stared at him.

'Cycled, Daddy?' enquired Joan. 'But you haven't got a bike.'

'There was one outside the pub,' he replied.

'Whose is it?' asked Joan.

Pierce thought about this for a moment and smiled. 'I haven't the foggiest,' he replied. 'I suppose I'd better take it back.'

The following week, another spectacle in the sky filled those who saw it with hope and wonder – including Annie and some of her daughters. Annie had been taking to her bed for increasingly long periods but on one of her better days, she decided that she could do with some fresh air. So she pushed Anne in her pram to the rec, where Kath, Sheila and Pat were playing with some friends.

On their way back home, something in the sky caught Kath's attention. She stopped and watched silently for a while, as clouds appeared to form a crucifix adorned with flowers, and a figure attached to it.

'Look! Look up there!' she shouted, and the others saw it too, to their astonishment. 'What is it, Mum?' she asked, feeling a little frightened of this apparition.

'I don't know,' Annie replied quietly, still staring at the image. All four of them now stood rooted to the spot as the image gently faded away.

A shiver ran down Annie's spine and she quickened her step on the way back to the house, hurrying the girls along with her.

'What was it, Mum?' asked Kath and Pat in turns. 'Was it a miracle?'

Annie just repeated that she didn't know and then said, 'Probably just clouds.' Even so, she felt unsettled by it. With the Blitz gaining momentum and the threat of a German invasion ever more present, the detail and clarity of the 'vision' were, in such difficult times, too great to be dismissed as nothing more than a natural cloud formation.

Back home, the girls told their sisters excitedly what they had seen, while Annie wondered if it really had been something extraordinary, or whether they had just been fanciful, imagining much more than was actually there. However, the following day they learnt that they were not the only people to have witnessed it. A headline in the

The Telegram

News Chronicle read 'Strangest Story of the War', and reported how a shepherd had been tending his sheep on the Sussex Downs when he noticed a white line spreading slowly across the sky:

> Gradually to his eyes it took the shape of Christ crucified on the Cross. Then six angels took form. The apparition lasted for two minutes, then faded. Mr Fowler rushed down the hillside to tell the village, and found he was not the only witness. Villagers working on the land said they had also seen it.

The Jarmans crowded around the paper. The article also quoted an evacuee named Mrs Steer, who had seen it along with her sister, Mrs Evans: 'We could see the nail in the crossed feet of Christ, and one of the angels with arms upstretched appeared to be praying.'

The report added that similar statements had been made by seven other villagers. Another newspaper, the *Southern Weekly News*, also carried an account from Mrs Steer. Like Annie, she had been unnerved:

> I happened to go outside my back door and noticed a white streak or road across the sky. Then gradually I saw a cross appear, standing upright, with Christ upon it. Shortly afterwards there were six angels on each side of him. It quite frightened me at first. I felt quite ill and I called my neighbour to look at it.

She also said that the figure of Christ had his head drooping to one side and remarked that the vision didn't seem to be a cloud formation as it didn't move. The image appeared gradually and then faded away slowly, lasting in all about two minutes.

The vision was a remarkable event in the Jarmans' eventful war that was to stay in their memories for ever.

As the end of 1940 approached, Pierce arrived in Hailsham one Friday evening looking shocked.

'I've got some awful news,' he told Annie. 'Dockhead Church has been bombed. It's been turned to rubble.'

As Catholics, Most Holy Trinity Church – as it was formally called – played a big part in the Jarmans' lives. It was where Annie and Pierce had got married and where they made sure their girls went to mass every Sunday.

'Is everyone OK?' she asked. 'Everyone safe?'

'Yes, no casualties,' Pierce reassured her. 'The convent is being used for mass.'

Having set the dockland area of the East End of London alight with their bombs, the Luftwaffe had recently switched their attention to the industrial Midlands and the North. Coventry was attacked by 449 bombers in a single night. Hull in Yorkshire suffered great damage. It was hard for Churchill or even Pathé News to put an upbeat spin on such devastation and loss of life. As the nation's backbone was put to the test, the Luftwaffe returned to London once more on 29 December, a Sunday night during the Christmas holiday, with the country's financial heartland, the City, as its target.

The area from Aldersgate to Cannon Street and Cheapside was set aflame, including nineteen churches, sixteen of which had been designed by Sir Christopher Wren after the Great Fire of London. However, a dramatic photograph in the following day's newspapers showed the dome of Wren's most famous building, St Paul's Cathedral, standing defiant and noble amongst the rubble, flames and smoke around it.

With the RAF denying the Luftwaffe air superiority over the South of England, Hitler postponed his plan to invade Britain in mid-September 1940, and turned his attention towards Russia. The bombing in London began to ease and, as it did so, Sheila's best friend, Mary Eddicott, broke some news to her that left Sheila feeling physically sick.

'We're going back to London,' she said at school playtime. She explained that her father had bought a greengrocer's shop in Tooley Street, and that she and her family were going to help run it. With planes being spotted overhead so frequently in Hailsham, the Eddicotts felt that the town was just as dangerous as London, so why not go home?

'If they can go back, why can't we?' a tearful Sheila asked her mother when she got home from school.

Annie put her arm around her daughter. 'We're safer here,' she said. However, even as she spoke, Annie's sadness at the prospect of losing her old friend Mary made her think that perhaps she and her daughters could return to Bermondsey too and be a complete family again. If only a house could be found for them. She discussed it with Pierce when he next visited.

'It's too dangerous, Annie,' Pierce told her. 'You've got to keep sheltering during the air raids. Where would you all go?'

Annie remonstrated with him, saying they would be near Stainer Street railway arch near London Bridge, which he had told her was being used as an ad hoc air-raid shelter. But Pierce held firm.

'There's nothing I'd like more than for us all to be back together again – but not if your lives are at risk.'

He was soon proved right. Not long after their conversation, Stainer Street arch suffered a direct hit on 17 February 1941. Sixty-eight people were killed, another 175 injured. For the time being, the Jarmans were staying put in Hailsham.

In any case, thought Pierce, Annie's fast-deteriorating health prevented the upheaval of leaving Hailsham to start afresh in London. To their dismay, Annie found she was coughing up blood again, and as she spent more frequent periods resting in bed, Joan was by now very capable with household chores. She made sure her younger sisters got off to school on time and provided meals, despite the challenge of more and more food becoming rationed.

When she sat beside her mother's bed, Mary felt too frightened to ask how she was. Annie understood, saying quietly, 'I know what's wrong. Don't worry.'

Hearing the words and seeing the sorrowful look on her mother's face made Mary panic. She didn't want to hear any more. 'You'll be all right, Mum,' she said quickly, adding, in an echo of Annie's reassurances in the past, 'just some rest is what you need.'

The local doctor had been called to visit on several occasions already, but the next time he came and examined Annie in bed, he told her that he was going to ring for an ambulance to take her into hospital. It wasn't to be just any old hospital, though. It was a specialist clinic for TB sufferers, many miles away from Hailsham and one she knew only too well – Grove Park. The thought of returning there filled Annie with dread, and she was distraught to think how far away from the girls she would be. This time, however, she was too weak to protest.

Mary was at work when the ambulance arrived and took Annie away but, knowing it was coming, she had kissed and hugged her mother goodbye that morning.

'I'll come and visit you at the weekend with Daddy,' Mary had said. 'Don't worry, Mum. You'll be better soon. They'll look after you in hospital, you'll see. Make you better and, before you know it, you'll be back here with us.'

The rest of the sisters were home when the ambulance arrived.

'Be good girls now, while I'm away,' Annie said weakly as she gave them all a hug and a kiss before being carried outside, her daughters trailing behind.

Kate stood in the doorway. 'Come inside now, girls,' she said, and they rushed upstairs to the bedroom overlooking the street where they could get a good view.

Crowded together at the window, trying not to cry, they looked out at their mother getting into the ambulance. Annie turned and waved, and they waved back. She saw her daughters' small faces framed in the window as she got into the vehicle and it drove away.

Joan choked back her emotion, not wanting her little sisters to know how worried she was, but tears rolled down Sheila's face freely as she stared at the empty space where the ambulance had been. She stayed frozen to the spot, long after the others had moved away. She had never seen her mother as bad as this.

Despite the fact that Annie's ill health meant that she had spent little time looking after the family in recent weeks and an increasing amount of time resting in bed, her absence from the house was very noticeable to the girls. With Pierce away working in London during the week, the sisters now felt their bond more closely than ever. They resolved to pull together and, in their mother's favourite words, 'not make a fuss'.

Mary continued to go to work and bring in some money, and life went on as well as it could. Annie was proud to hear it when Pierce visited her in hospital and spoke about how they were getting along.

But all of the girls were subdued. Kath and Pat were not so full of high jinks and Sheila retreated into herself even more, finding solace in books, now that her mother and her best friend were no longer around. Pierce too had lost his spark, which was noticeable to the girls when he arrived at the weekends.

Despite all of this, the girls comforted themselves in their belief that Annie would be out of hospital and back home with them soon – as had happened before. Even Mary and Joan, who had discussed the seriousness of their mother's condition between themselves, thought this would be the case. Going to bed at night in the dark and quiet countryside during a war, without a mother or father around, was frightening, and the younger girls huddled together, reassuring themselves with talk of Annie's recovery.

There had always been a night-time buzz of noise from the streets back in Bermondsey, especially after pub closing time. However, here in Hailsham all was quiet, and the blackout curtains prevented the moon from offering any illumination inside their bedroom. Sometimes, if they awoke in the small hours, the girls would temporarily think they had gone blind, and if they needed to use the precariously positioned toilet it took a concerted effort to feel their way there. The less adventurous sisters would light a candle but this frequently attracted complaints from their roommates.

Even though Annie loved her girls so much and worried constantly about them during her stay in hospital, she didn't want them to visit her and see how poorly she was. Pierce told his daughters that it was best to leave their mother to rest for the time being and for them to 'do her proud' at home but, worried about her frailty and fearing the worst, he eventually persuaded Annie to let Mary accompany him on his next visit.

Mary was shocked to see how pale and weak her mother looked, lying there in bed. Annie was clearly having trouble breathing but did her best to communicate. She was eager to hear all the news and gossip from Hailsham and to find out how each of her daughters was doing. Mary recounted as much as she could, and even made Annie smile when she told her that Miss Hunt was still giving them cakes and pies. Even though she had been pleased to see her mother, on the train back home to Hailsham Mary, who by nature enjoyed a laugh, felt an aching sorrow. Little was said between father and daughter. Neither was much in the mood for conversation.

Back in the hospital, Annie, who had put on such a brave face for her husband and daughter, shed a tear once they had gone. Lying there, in that foreboding place to which she had hoped never to return, she longed to be back in the countryside – anywhere but the hospital – with her girls. It all seemed so far away now. She tried to think nice thoughts – of the happy times she had spent with her family both in Hailsham and Bermondsey – but each time she heard a moan or a rasping cough from a neighbouring bed, the words of that young lad who had carried her suitcase to the hospital gates four years earlier echoed in her head: 'I didn't think anyone ever walked out of this hospital.'

Much to the girls' displeasure, after a few weeks of Annie being in hospital, their aunts moved in to live with them at Battle Road. The three women did little to contribute to the running of the house, and the girls' elderly grandmother was not up to taking on anything too strenuous, so it was Joan who bore the brunt of the domestic work.

The aunts were certainly no substitute for the firm but loving Annie. They lacked the emotional skills of comfort, understanding and compassion the children needed in the absence of their mother's care. Despite their comparative wealth, the aunts never bought the girls any treats either, not even sweets, and they could be very blunt and tactless, seemingly unaware of the family's troubles.

'I don't think they want to look after us at all,' Sheila said crossly to Joan as they were carrying some groceries back from the shop one day. 'They just want to get away from the bombs. They know it's safer down here.'

'Well, maybe it's just their way,' said Joan, wise beyond her years and wondering how her mother would reply. Secretly she suspected her younger sister was right, and she knew Mary felt the same.

One evening, when they were sitting in the front room with their aunts, Joan, Mary and Sheila started talking about when they thought their mother would return. Nell, who had been reading a book, looked up and said bluntly, 'She's not coming home.' The girls were shocked. Why would she say such a horrid thing?

'She is coming home!' Sheila shouted, with tears in her

eyes. 'She's going to get better. She *is* coming home!' And she stormed out of the room.

Joan went after her and comforted her in their bedroom, telling her not to take any notice. 'You know what they're like,' she added.

However, two weeks went by and there was still no sign of their mother returning.

On a sunny day that June, Kath caught up with Sheila as she walked the short distance back home from school for lunch. They chatted away merrily as they walked down the side path and into the kitchen.

Inside, Sheila caught sight of Aunt Nell standing at the sink, peeling potatoes. 'Oh, Aunt, they won't be ready in time,' she said apologetically. 'We've only got an hour for lunch.'

Nell looked over her shoulder and replied brusquely, 'Well, you'll just have to wait, won't you?'

Sheila then noticed Joan, who was standing quietly nearby, looking at her with a solemn expression on her face and holding a sheet of paper in her hand, a telegram. Sheila – always the most intuitive of the sisters – felt a sudden chill. Something was wrong and, somehow, she knew what it was.

Now Nell turned fully towards Sheila and Kath and, wiping her wet hands on her apron, said simply, 'Your mum's dead.'

Annie died on 12 June 1941, at the age of forty-seven, four years after being told by a doctor that she only had ten months to live. Pierce, despite knowing that she was living on borrowed time, was a broken man, and the girls – Mary, sixteen; Joan, fourteen; Sheila, eleven; Kath, nine; Pat, seven; and Anne, two – were shattered to have lost their beloved mum.

CHAPTER 5

All for One

Pierce with his daughters in the garden at 18 Battle Road. Back (from left to right) Joan and Sheila; front (from left to right) Pat, Anne and Kath.

THE BRUTAL ANNOUNCEMENT of Annie's death was all Aunt Nell offered her young charges. There were no words of comfort, no hugs.

There was the briefest of pauses before the silence was broken by a scream. 'No!' yelled Sheila. 'No! No, she isn't!'

Kath, too stunned to take it in, stood in confused silence.

It was Joan who came over to comfort her sisters and to show them the telegram that Pierce had sent to Nell from London, informing them of Annie's death. The truth was there in black and white, and yet there was a pervading feeling of disbelief amongst the girls because each of them, Mary aside, truly believed that their mother would get well and return home to them, despite their worries. She had always battled illness and refused to let it conquer her. She loved them and wouldn't want to leave them.

Mary had been the only one to see her so poorly in hospital and in her private thoughts she had feared that her mother would die.

'I'll tell your teachers that you're too upset to return to school this afternoon,' said Nell calmly.

Sheila took herself off to the bedroom where she looked out of the window – the same window through which she had last seen her mother being taken away in the ambulance a month earlier. She watched the other children walking back to school after lunchtime and, as much as she disliked school, she wished with all her heart that she too was going back there right now, because that would mean that everything was all right, everything was normal.

Kath and Pat went off to the garden to try to get away from the oppressive atmosphere in the house. They looked out over to the fields, seeing through their tearful eyes the cows in the distance, the same cows they had first seen when they arrived at Battle Road and couldn't wait to tell their mother about.

'Who will look after us?' asked Pat eventually.

'Joan,' said Kath without any hesitation, cuffing her running nose. 'And Daddy, of course. We don't need anyone else.'

Mary was the last of the girls to learn of Annie's death when she returned home from work that evening and, like her sisters, she was devastated by the news.

'I can't take it in,' she said when she was alone with Joan for a while in the front room.

'Did you think she was that bad?' asked Joan.

'She was bad but . . . well, she's Mum,' Mary replied. 'She's always bounced back.'

As both of them shed tears, an angry Mary cried through her sobs, 'God is so cruel! How can he take her away from us?' and they cuddled each other in an effort to shut out the painful reality.

The house was unusually quiet that evening, save for the sound of sobbing.

When Pierce arrived the next day, the girls noticed how red-rimmed his eyes were and how ashen-faced he was, despite his best attempt to be strong in front of them. It was clear that he had been crying, and it took a lot of willpower to prevent his grief from overflowing once more as he embraced his girls.

'Mummy would want us to stay strong,' he said in a faltering voice. 'We need to do her proud. She's at rest now.'

Sheila, acutely feeling the loss of her mother, now hated Hailsham more than ever and longed to return home to Bermondsey. In the afternoon, Aunt Rose asked her to help with some shopping in the High Street but Sheila didn't want to go. She was so grief stricken that she just wanted to hide herself away in the house. Her eyes were red and sore from crying, and she didn't want anyone to see her, but she did as she was asked.

'Please don't stop to talk to anyone,' she urged her aunt.

'I have to be polite,' Rose replied, as insensitive as ever.

Sheila just wanted to get back to the house as quickly as possible. Rose was in no hurry, though, stopping for a lengthy chat in the High Street with a woman who knew Annie. Rose talked about Annie's death in her usual matter-of-fact manner while a distraught Sheila stood by with tears rolling down her face.

'I didn't want you to stop to talk,' she said when they were finally walking home again.

'I told you, Sheila,' Rose snapped, 'you've got to be polite. You would do well to remember that.'

Sheila thought to herself, as she walked, that all three of their aunts were not the slightest bit upset about her mother's death. They had never liked her. Now she understood why the aunts had come to stay: to be with them while Pierce was at Annie's bedside. But she didn't want them around for a moment longer.

*

Pierce had thought it best that only Mary, as the eldest of the sisters, should attend the funeral back in London. It would be too upsetting for the younger girls and Joan needed to stay at home to look after them. They were secretly relieved. They had dreaded the idea of attending. Mary didn't want to go either but she thought it too insensitive to tell her father and, in any case, he needed her support.

A few days before the funeral, Pierce and Mary, along with Tom and Kate, travelled up to London on the train. With the family home having been bombed, they all stayed at the aunts' house where, in the living room, Mary saw the familiar glass bowl of boiled sweets.

'Have a sweet, Mary,' said Rose, who saw her looking. Mary took one, once more wondering why they were happy to share sweets and cakes with them in their own house but never thought to bring some down to Hailsham. Indeed, when Annie was unable to afford the family ration of sweets, or bacon and other tasty treats, the aunts would use it for themselves and take it back home with them to Bermondsey.

Before the war, Mary would often visit her aunts on a Sunday – not so much for their company but because she got to eat some of their sweets and fresh fruit, which the Jarmans didn't have at home, along with a filling meal.

The downside was that after tea – a slice of cake and soft drink for Mary – the aunts had their traditional nap in the double bed they all shared, despite there being two spare bedrooms. Although used to sharing a bed with her sisters, Mary thought it very odd that her aunts, at their age, did the same thing. They insisted that Mary join them, saying it would do her good to rest. She hated lying on that bed, wide awake and squashed between her aunts, while they all slept, and she would have to wait until they awoke before she could get up herself.

It was usual for Irish Catholic families to have a wake, with the body of the deceased lying in rest in the family house for a few days prior to the funeral, so that wider family, friends and neighbours could say goodbye. However, because London was still being bombed and regular air-raid sirens meant that people had to rush to shelter, the custom had been suspended. They did have Annie's body at the aunts' house the night before the funeral, though, when luckily no air-raid siren sounded, and a few friends and neighbours called to pay their respects, share a drink and reminisce about life with Annie. There was some laughter between the tears at some of the anecdotes, which was a welcome relief.

The coffin was placed in one of the spare bedrooms. Mary could scarcely believe that her lively, forceful mother was now lying inside that box behind the closed door. She felt scared each time she passed by the room and hurried along, trying not to think about what was inside.

As the adults chatted quietly amongst themselves in the front room, Mary's thoughts turned towards Annie's rather irrational dislike of the local undertaker, Fred 'Freddie' Albin.

'He's a show-off,' she would say to whomever was listening, whenever she saw him walking slowly in front of a funeral procession, top hat in hand and carrying a cane. 'I'm not having him burying me.'

Pierce was amused and the girls bemused at why she took so against him, as he appeared to be no different from any other undertaker putting on a show for the mourners. But she was adamant.

'I don't want him walking in front of me with his hat and stick in his hand, showing off,' she would say.

On the morning of Annie's funeral, however, three horse-drawn carriages turned up at the aunts' house and out of one stepped an immaculately dressed Freddie Albin, top hat perched on his head and cane in his hand.

'I thought Mummy didn't want Freddie Albin,' Mary whispered to her father as they stood in the doorway whilst neighbours gathered nearby, in traditional fashion, to pay their respects.

'We had to have him,' Pierce replied in hushed tones. 'He buries all Dockhead people.'

Mary imagined her mother's annoyance at not getting her own way. On top of it all was the way Pierce was dressed. Annie would have snatched the black bowler off his head had she been alive to see it. He had bought it for the funeral of a friend and she had hated it so much that she had buried it in the back of the wardrobe so that he wouldn't find it. Joan had seen her making space for it and had asked what she was doing.

'Hiding that bloomin' bowler!' Annie had cried. 'It looks ridiculous on him. And if he asks where it is, you don't know.'

Now, that vivacious woman, full of life and opinions and love, was being hoisted onto her funeral carriage in her coffin. Immediate family climbed into the two other carriages and the procession made its way slowly to what remained of their old house in Abbey Street, preceded by Freddie Albin, walking solemnly with top hat in one hand, cane in the other.

The procession stopped for a couple of minutes outside the bomb-damaged house and Mary, looking out of the carriage window, saw many recognizable faces as their old neighbours bowed their heads by the roadside. Then, Freddie got into one of the carriages and they made their way to St Patrick's Roman Catholic Cemetery in Leytonstone, the usual East London final resting place for the deceased Catholics of Dockhead.

They crossed the river Thames at Tower Bridge and on both sides, friends and complete strangers alike stopped in the street as a sign of respect, men doffing their hats and caps, and several making the sign of the cross as the procession passed by.

Alighting at the cemetery, they were taken into the small chapel, which Mary thought was a damp, miserable little place, not good enough for her mother. The coffin was brought in and the priest said a few words – none of which Mary listened to, as she felt too emotionally numb to take much in. Everything just seemed so unreal. The family knelt and said their private prayers before Annie was buried in the rather crowded cemetery amongst many other freshly dug graves, victims of the Blitz.

As the coffin was lowered into the ground, grief overwhelmed Mary and her tears flowed freely but Pierce was intent on holding his emotions in check. Away from his daughter and family, he'd already shed many private tears and was finding it hard to imagine a life without his wonderful Annie. Mary thought her father's behaviour more than a little odd, though, particularly when he turned to her after the burial and remarked, in what appeared to be a matter-of-fact way, 'Well, that's the last you'll see of your mum.' It was a response that was greatly out of character, leaving Mary deeply concerned for her father's wellbeing.

The funeral had been such an ordeal – Pierce was only glad that his younger daughters had been spared the experience. However, it was difficult to know what was more traumatic – being there or not getting the chance to say goodbye. Back in Hailsham that day, Joan did her best to carry on with life as normal, getting the younger girls ready for school and trying not to think about the funeral happening in London. During the day she busied herself by cleaning the house and taking Anne out for some fresh air.

For Sheila, Kath and Pat, it was difficult to concentrate on school lessons or to talk to anyone other than themselves. They alone had the shared experiences with their mother; they alone knew the pain they were feeling. They yearned for the school day to end so that they could return home and not have to try to put on brave faces any longer. However, once back at the house, the haunting memories and unusual quietness did nothing to alleviate their suffering and, of course, Annie's much-loved possessions all around the house served as constant reminders of her presence *and* absence – the photographs, her perfume, hairbrush and the clock with its regal chime.

Pierce, Annie's parents and the aunts all remained in London for a few days after the funeral but Mary wanted desperately to return to Hailsham and to her sisters, and so she made her own way back to the countryside on a Green Line bus from London Bridge. She stared out of the dirty window, seeing nothing, her vision blurred by tears and her mind filled with a confusion of thoughts, emotions and memories.

She remembered the happy time, just before they were evacuated, when she and her sisters had finally persuaded their mother to let them go 'hopping'. This was an excursion to the Kent countryside at the end of summer each year to pick hops for the manufacture of beer. It was regarded by underprivileged Londoners as a working holiday – the only type they could afford. An added attraction for children was that the season started in September, which meant they would have an extra four weeks off school after the long summer break.

The girls had envied some of their friends who had been taken hopping in previous years and yearned to go themselves but Annie had always resisted. She may have had to scrimp and scrape all her life to make the pennies stretch but she was a proud woman and felt that she had enough to do at home, bringing up her large family. She wasn't overjoyed at the idea of decamping to the countryside for four weeks either, living in very basic conditions and doing what she had heard was hard, dirty work. Besides, it would mean being away from Pierce.

However, when Mrs Gardner, who lived across the road, invited Annie and her daughters to share a hopping bin with her in September 1938, Annie, after talking it over with Pierce, relented. 'It will be a bit of extra money,' he told Annie. 'And a holiday for the girls.'

Although there were trains from London Bridge, known as 'hoppers' specials', the Bermondsey families opted to share a lorry down to the countryside in order to take more luggage and a few home comforts they suspected they'd need.

On the day they were due to travel, all of the girls were up early and soon milling around outside the house, bursting with anticipation and waiting to catch sight of the vehicle. Although the drive from London to Kent was a long and uncomfortable one, crammed into the back of the lorry and sitting on the floor as there were no seats, they spent much of the journey in high spirits, singing 'hopping songs' that had been passed down through the generations. A favourite had many verses and slight variations of the lyrics from family to family, but the Jarmans soon picked it up:

If you go down hopping, hopping down in Kent,
You'll see old Mother Riley a-putting up her tent.
With a tee-aye-o, tee-aye-o, tee-aye-ee-aye-o.

They say that hopping's lousy, I don't believe it's true,
We only go down hopping to earn a bob or two.
With a tee-aye-o, tee-aye-o, tee-aye-ee-aye-o.

Annie and the girls took up residence in one of the wooden huts where the beds were just benches covered with straw. Annie, determined to make things as nice as possible – as always – placed sheets over the beds but, even so, the scratchy straw was horribly uncomfortable and poked through the sheets, irritating their skin. The other furniture consisted of a table and some chairs, and cooking had to be done outside over a campfire – to all intents and purposes, they were camping. Annie, who so enjoyed her creature comforts, couldn't believe what she'd signed up to. This was certainly nowhere near to her usual standards.

Soon after they got there, the girls were sent off to gather twigs with the rest of the children. Whatever they brought back was amassed and lit and, when it had burned down to grey ashes, cooking began. Annie copied the other mums, chopping up vegetables and putting them in a pan of water to hang from a rod, resting on two makeshift tripods, over the ashes. Water for tea was boiled in the same way. It was basic but exciting for the girls and they all agreed – even Annie – that everything seemed to taste much better than at home.

After an uncomfortable night's sleep they were woken bright and early by the farm manager and taken directly to the hop farm where each family was allocated a bin – a rectangular-shaped piece of sacking that was carried along the field as hops were picked, stripped of their leaves and thrown into it. The girls were keen to help initially, but very soon realized that their new 'game' came with an element they weren't so keen on – work.

Mary felt herself smiling through her pain as she sat on the Green Line bus, remembering how she had complained to her mother that the smell of the hops made her feel sick. After further moaning and complaining from her other daughters, Annie sent them off to play. Their hop-picking duties were over for the rest of their stay but Annie didn't mind in the least. For her, the most important thing was that her girls had a wonderful time.

After a hard day's work picking hops, the women would sit around the fire, talking and sometimes singing. At the weekends, Pierce, along with other husbands and fathers, caught the train down from London to join their families. Then, in the early evening, the adults would spend an hour or two chatting and singing in the local pub. The prospect of war was a recurring theme of their conversation and Annie, along with some of the other mums, felt sure that if war broke out, the farmer would let them stay there, even though he hadn't remotely suggested or indicated such a thing.

'We're good workers, earning a living and making him money,' Annie had said. 'Why wouldn't he want us?' Then, looking around her, taking in the healthy faces, bronzed from their exertions in the sunshine, she had added, 'I'd feel safe here.'

With Annie now buried at Leytonstone, at peace in her final resting place, a few days after the funeral Pierce made his way to Hailsham on a bus, along with his sisters. The girls went to meet them in the High Street at the Green Line office. Despite her sadness, Joan had a wry smile when she saw her dad because he was wearing the black bowler hat that Annie had so detested. She wondered how he had managed to find it.

In a quiet moment alone with his daughters, Pierce talked to them about the future. 'You know that I need to carry on working in London,' he said. 'And that means that I can't be with you. Of course, I'll be here every weekend but . . . ' Here he took a deep breath. 'I think it best if your aunts stayed with you.'

He'd already discussed it with his sisters and they had agreed, but Pierce knew what the reaction was likely to be from his daughters. Predictably, the girls, as one, were horrified by this arrangement. Their aunts had always been found lacking in their affections towards their nieces, but never more so than in the aftermath of Annie's death.

'We'll be fine, Daddy,' said Joan. 'We can look after ourselves.'

'Yes,' agreed Mary. 'We don't need anyone during the week. We've been managing pretty much on our own anyway.'

'I can cook and get the girls ready for school,' said Joan. 'And shop.'

'We can do everything on our own,' added Kath helpfully.

Pierce looked at his daughters fondly, feeling proud of seeing Annie's resilient spirit in them.

'And who's going to look after the baby while you're at school and work?' he asked. They were silenced for a moment, not knowing what to say.

'I'll be leaving school in a few months' time,' said Joan. 'I can look after her all day then and run the house. I know what to do.'

Pierce smiled. He knew that was true. He looked at his daughters' imploring faces and felt a rush of sadness and compassion that threatened to choke him.

'Maybe your aunts can stay just until you leave school, Joan,' he said, turning swiftly away. 'But I'll need to discuss things with the welfare officer.'

Their evacuation had delayed Kath making her First Holy Communion in Bermondsey and so she made it in Hailsham with Pat, and a group of other girls and boys, in that summer of 1941.

The two girls had looked forward eagerly to the day because it was such a special occasion. They got to dress up in white dresses with veils, like little brides, while their families looked on lovingly as they walked down the church aisle. The fact that their mother wouldn't be there to fuss over them on their big day, and that Pierce was working in London and unable to get away, cast a dark shadow over their excitement. Mary had wondered if she could afford to buy the material to make them dresses but a local lady named Mrs Jenner, who had known Annie well, took pity on the girls and made beautiful white dresses and veils for them to wear. When they tried them on at home for the first time, their faces lit up with joy.

'Don't they look pretty, Pat?' said Kath. She twirled around in her dress in front of the long wooden mirror in the bedroom, as Mrs Jenner helped Pat into hers.

'It's the best dress *ever*,' said Pat breathlessly, copying her sister's twirls.

Joan looked on, smiling. 'Thank you so much, Mrs Jenner,' she said.

Her thanks were echoed by her excited sisters before Mrs Jenner advised that they take the dresses off straight away and hang them in the wardrobe to keep them clean and crease-free for the big day. Grudgingly, Pat and Kath were helped out of their dresses and Joan hung them up, away from harm's reach.

After Mrs Jenner had left, Kath and Pat couldn't help sneaking looks at their outfits. They had never owned anything so beautiful in their young lives. As delighted as they were, though, they couldn't help but think wistfully how much their mother would have liked to have been there for the occasion. She would have been proud that they looked so pretty and weren't 'shown up', as she would have put it, by the other girls.

The evening before the service, the children due to make their Communion went to St Wilfrid's Church to confess their sins to Father Frost. Then, the following morning, Kath and Pat could barely wait to get into their dresses.

'Don't rush, girls. You don't want to tear anything,' Aunt Rose warned as she watched them. The girls were untypically careful as they tried to keep their immaculate dresses clean.

Getting ready for work that morning, Mary recalled her

own First Holy Communion back in Bermondsey. She had also worn a white dress and veil, and had felt very special. As they had sung the traditional hymn 'Jesus, Thou Art Coming', she had believed passionately that He was indeed coming to her and the others on that day. After the service, they had made their way from Most Holy Trinity Church to their school, for a breakfast of soft-boiled egg and bread soldiers.

Mary was fortunate enough to have had her mother with her then but now it was Joan and Aunt Rose who accompanied Kath and Pat to St Wilfrid's, along with little Anne, who sat on Rose's lap. Like Mary before them, the girls joined in enthusiastically with the hymn and then walked proudly down the aisle in line, hands pressed together in prayer, until it was their turn to see Father Frost hold aloft a communion wafer.

'The body of Christ,' he said.

Kath and Pat, like all the children, were well rehearsed about every aspect of the ceremony. They replied 'Amen' dutifully, then opened their mouths wide for the priest to place a wafer on their tongue. They then bowed their heads and walked slowly back to their seats, letting the wafer dissolve in their mouths, just as they had been told to. Kath felt hers sticking to the roof of her mouth and desperately wanted to dislodge it. They had been warned not to touch the wafer with their fingers though, so, on the way back to her seat, she tried to use her tongue to release it instead.

'Why on earth is Kath pulling such funny faces?' whispered Aunt Rose to Joan.

'I don't know – but trust her to spoil the look,' Joan replied, with a motherly shake of the head.

*

That same summer saw Joan embarking on a new chapter in life when she left school, aged fourteen. Like her sister before her, she got a job at the Silverlight Laundry, working on a giant wringer with huge rollers. She and some of the other women would feed wet sheets into one side of the machine, which would be squeezed of water before emerging from the other side. It was a rather monotonous routine and lifting wet sheets was quite tiring, but she enjoyed the company of her work colleagues and felt relieved to be free from the pressure of school. What's more, she was now being treated as an adult.

Joan and Mary hadn't stopped pressurizing their father to let them care for their sisters without the foreboding presence of their aunts.

'I can give up work and look after the baby,' said Joan, who had had quite enough of handling heavy wet sheets already.

Eventually, Pierce visited the local welfare officer to discuss the possibility of his girls living in the house on their own. Faced with mild opposition, he found himself making assurances that his daughters were perfectly capable of looking after themselves. In the end, convinced by Pierce's arguments, the welfare officer replied that he was happy for them to give it a go, saying he would keep an eye on them and that, so long as they were able to manage, the arrangement would be fine.

The girls were delighted when Pierce told them the news but he repeated what the welfare officer had said and warned them that the smallest thing – even a row – might get reported to the authorities, and they'd no longer be able to live together without their aunts.

Tom and Kate were also preparing to move back to

Bermondsey, into a new house that had been found for them. However, Pierce explained that they, along with the aunts, would still visit and stay with the girls from time to time, just to keep an eye on things. Of course, he would be down at weekends too. In truth, the girls didn't really need his reassurances, though – they were determined to succeed and their already close bond became even tighter.

Joan gave up working at the Silverlight Laundry once her aunts and grandparents had returned to Bermondsey and took on her mother's role in earnest, looking after her sisters, feeding them, shopping, and doing household chores. On warm days she would wheel little Anne to the rec in her pram and mix with the mothers there. Caring for such a young child was a big responsibility and she felt it keenly. However, some of the mothers at the rec, who had known Annie well, kept an eye on how Joan was doing and kindly offered advice as well as enquiring how baby Anne was faring.

The Jarmans' neighbours were very helpful too, touched by the fact that the girls had lost their mother. Rosie Goldsmith, next door, looked out for them and Miss Hunt stepped up her home baking . . .

Mrs Gates, the lady who owned the Silverlight Laundry, even told Mary to cram the family's dirty washing into a pillow case every week and it would be cleaned in the laundry for free, which was a big help to Joan.

Slowly they became accustomed to life without Annie, but there were many tearful times when the terrible loss of a mother, one who had always seemed to know what to say and do, became unbearable. The girls had inherited her strong spirit and resilience but nevertheless they sorely missed having a mother to turn to for comfort and advice about the problems each of them were facing at the various stages of their lives.

They coped on their own admirably, for the most part. However, Pierce's caution to his girls about being on their best behaviour went unheeded one day when Joan, who managed the purse strings tightly, felt that she had a few pennies to spare for a rare treat of some sweets for her sisters.

Kath was excited at being asked to be the one to buy them, and she hurried along to Bainbridge's shop on the corner of Battle Road to carry out her duties. Inside the store, her mouth watered at the sight and smell of the colourful confectionery on display.

'Can I have a quarter of sherbet lemons, please?' she asked the elderly Mr Bainbridge.

As he moved towards the jar of sweets, he noticed that it needed topping up. 'I just have to pop out the back to get some more,' he said to Kath.

In the few moments while he was gone, Kath, alone in the shop, had a sudden urge that she couldn't resist. Without really thinking, she found herself reaching over the counter to steal a small square packet of chewing gum, which she put in her pocket quickly before Mr Bainbridge came back.

Kath felt the blood rush to her face and a roaring in her ears seemed to drown out all other noise when Mr Bainbridge returned. She was certain that he could tell, just by looking at her, what she had done. She couldn't look him in the eye and handed over the money for the sherbet lemons swiftly before making a hasty exit, feeling a knot in her stomach as she walked out of the door. As she made her way along the street, she felt certain that everyone was looking at her burning face, aware of her crime. To make matters worse, she noticed the police station immediately opposite Bainbridge's. What if someone came out and started questioning her, and found the gum in her pocket? They would arrest her, for sure. What would Joan say? What would Daddy say? Worse yet, what would her mother have said?

She would have to get rid of the evidence. So, moving away from the scene of the crime as fast as she could, she took the chewing gum from her pocket surreptitiously and put each little square into her mouth at the same time. Finding a bin, she threw away the wrapper and chewed so voraciously that her jaw ached. At the next bin, she took the mangled gum out of her mouth and threw it in. Her heart was still thumping when she reached her house and she spent the rest of the evening worrying that the police would come rapping on the door at any moment.

Kath avoided returning to Bainbridge's for as long as she could but, weeks later, she was sent there on an errand by Joan. The idea was to push Anne there in her pram so that she could get some fresh air and maybe fall asleep. Arriving at the shop, Kath left Anne outside in the pram for a couple of minutes while she went inside. When she emerged, sweets in hand, Kath walked off cheerfully towards home, back along Battle Road and into the house. In the kitchen, Joan looked curiously at Kath.

'What?' asked Kath. 'Why are you looking at me like that?' This time, she wasn't guilty of theft. Her conscience was clear.

'Where's the baby?' Joan asked.

Kath looked puzzled.

'Where's Anne?' said Joan, with mounting anxiety.

Kath froze, her eyes wide and mouth open. Then, she hurtled out of the door and ran full pelt down the road back to Bainbridge's. There, to her great relief, she found Anne still outside in her pram, and fast asleep.

Sheila's closeness to her mother made the pain of her loss particularly deep. Her sisters had always called her the apple of her mother's eye and, back in Bermondsey, Kath used to look on enviously as Annie curled Sheila's hair patiently into cascading ringlets every morning.

'Can you do mine like that, Mum?' she would ask.

'Your hair isn't long enough, darling,' Annie would reply.

For six months after Annie's death, Sheila had nightmares in which her mother wasn't really dead at all. Instead, she was living back in London with their father because she no longer wanted to leave him on his own. The girls had only been told that Annie had died because she didn't want them to think that she had abandoned them. In her sleep, Sheila would feel comforted that her mum was really alive and that she would see her again once the war was over and they could return to their life in Bermondsey. But then she would wake up, sweating on a damp bedsheet, and realize that she had been tossing and turning with the emotional turmoil of her dream. In that neverland, where the dream state permeates reality, for a moment she would be unsure whether her mother was really dead or alive. And then she would remember.

Sheila never talked to anyone about her dreams and, by keeping them to herself, she could almost convince herself that what she had dreamt was true. In any case, she felt that there was no one she could confide in – they simply wouldn't understand.

All for One

Without her mother, she felt a wave of sadness each time she put her own hair into ringlets, missing the chats and laughs she used to have with Annie, telling her about things going on at school. She missed the protectiveness that only a mother can provide. What she didn't know was that Joan – the most practical and mature of the sisters – was also experiencing very similar nightmares about their mother being alive back in Bermondsey. Like Sheila, she felt too foolish to tell anyone about them, and so they endured their anguish individually when they might have found comfort in each other.

Joan also felt the pressure and sadness of having to be mum to others, when she dearly wanted one for herself. While Mary was at work and the others at school, at home Joan was reminded of Annie constantly in every domestic task she undertook. While she could offer reassurance to her younger sisters, there was no motherly figure to look after *her*; to listen to her concerns and offer advice and comfort. Whether it was lining up for food at the shops, taking her younger sisters to school or Anne to the park, Joan found herself amongst real mums – women – much older than herself, and she felt out of place and lonely.

Her feelings were brought to the forefront of her mind when she went to watch Kath and Pat competing at the school sports day at the rec. Joan, holding Anne on her lap, was sitting on a bench with a group of evacuee mothers from London when one of the teachers announced that it was time for the mums' race.

A few game contenders stood up. While there was a general reticence amongst the London mums, they gave plenty of encouragement to Joan, who was taken aback.

'No, I'm not doing it,' she said. 'I'm not a mum.'

'Yes, you are. As good as,' one of them replied.

Joan still felt awkward but, after further encouragement, she got up and took her place with several others on the starting line. As she was considerably younger than the other runners, she won the race with ease and was cheered back to her seat, but she felt neither victorious nor happy. And she didn't feel like a mum. She was only fourteen years old and she should have been cheering on her *own* mum. She missed Annie desperately.

Mary had the distraction of work and of seeing a variety of people to help take her mind off the sadness that now enveloped the sisters every time they entered 18 Battle Road. She enjoyed interacting with the different people she met on her round. She loved to stop for a chat. At school in Dockhead, her teacher, Sister Bonaventure, had labelled her Miss Busybody because she was always turning around in class to talk to people. Eventually, the exasperated teacher had told her to sit at the back of the class so that there would be nobody behind for her to turn to. This suited Mary just fine because she could then talk as much as she liked to the girls sitting either side of her, so long as she used the girl in front as a shield. It wasn't to last, though. One day, she pushed things too far by putting her feet up on her desk, confident that Sister Bonaventure couldn't see her. She was right. However, the headmistress, Sister Fidelis, could see her very clearly indeed as she made her daily visit to Mary's classroom and peered through the glass window in the door.

When Mary caught sight of the nun, she tried hurriedly to get her legs down but it was too late. Sister Fidelis, who had a penchant for coming up with novel and effective forms of punishment, had already worked out what she would do.

'No, Mary Jarman,' she said in a loud voice, making the whole class freeze in fear. 'If you're feeling tired, then you would be better to sit like that all day.'

Everyone was amazed by how kind Sister Fidelis was being but they soon realized – none more so than Mary herself – how much feet and legs could ache in a raised position. After Sister Fidelis had left, Mary's teacher let her suffer for a while before making her switch seats with a girl in the front row. There Mary stayed for the rest of the term, under Sister Bonaventure's watchful eye.

Now, during the course of her job on the open road, Mary loved the chance to chat, her freedom and the fact that she didn't have an employer breathing down her neck. After a very traumatic and difficult time, it was a pleasure to be back at work.

One of her customers had a beautiful collie dog which Mary would often admire. The woman told Mary that the dog was pregnant and that there would soon be lots of puppies around. On subsequent visits, Mary would enquire how the dog was and sometimes she would bend over to stroke the collie as she sat quietly in her basket. She found it soothing. When the litter of puppies arrived Mary thought they were the cutest things she had ever seen – light brown in colour and soft to the touch, they lay curled up, with their eyes squeezed tightly shut to the outside world.

'Oh, aren't they gorgeous!' Mary said, all gooey-eyed. 'They're just like balls of fluff!'

The woman laughed, then, to Mary's amazement, said to her, 'When they're a bit bigger, you can have one, if you like.'

Mary looked at her, not quite believing her ears. 'Really?' she asked.

The woman nodded. 'If you can give it a good home.'

'Oh, yes,' said Mary. 'We'll take good care of it.'

The woman kept her word, and a couple of months later Mary proudly took one of the puppies home to Battle Road. She named it Paddy. Her sisters were very excited to have a dog of their own but the younger ones sometimes got frightened when it scampered around their feet and pawed at their legs. Kath and Pat weren't used to dogs – Abbey Street had never felt big enough for one, and Annie wouldn't have liked the mess anyway – and so they would scream and jump onto a chair to escape. The more they screamed, the more the puppy scampered.

With no idea how to train the dog, it ran around the house and garden, eliciting frequent squeals from the girls. Eventually, frustrated by the noise and disruption, their granddad took it upon himself to train the pup. However, Mary was quite alarmed when she saw him smack it. Although it wasn't a hard blow and, in Tom's mind, nothing more than a reasonable reproof to teach the dog right from wrong, Mary took it to heart. Paddy was her dog, after all.

She rushed outside. 'Stop it! You mustn't hit him!' she cried, scooping Paddy up in her arms and cuddling him.

'It needs to be taught obedience,' her granddad replied crossly. 'It's not hurt. But you have to show it who is master.'

Nevertheless, Mary vowed that he would never hit Paddy again. She was aware, though, that the dog was somewhat out of control, scaring her younger sisters as well as irritating her grandparents and aunts. Plus, it was another mouth to feed during a time of rationing and hardship. So, after talking it over with her sisters and a lot of heartache, Mary decided to give Paddy away. She found him a good home nearby with one of the other evacuee mums from Bermondsey, Mrs Arnold. The girls saw him being walked from time to time and thought he looked just like Lassie, the canine star of the feel-good family movies . . . and now that he was no longer in their care, was just as well behaved!

As well as her work at the laundry, Mary had another distraction which helped to take her mind off the loss of Annie. Her assistant, Iris, had got her interested in dancing and they would go to Polegate or nearby Magham Down several times a week. With a dearth of eligible young British men on home shores, the Canadian soldiers in Hailsham, along with a smattering of Americans nearby, were very popular at local dance nights.

The girls would don their best dresses, and the dressmaking skills that Mary had learnt at Koupy Gowns were put to good use as she made her own outfits at a fraction of the price they cost to buy. As was the fashion, Mary and Iris would apply 'liquid stockings' and then draw a line up the back of each other's legs with an eyeliner pencil to replicate the stocking seam.

At the dance nights, a small band played tunes to suit a variety of popular dances, from the waltz to the foxtrot and the jitterbug, and included such favourites as 'Apple Blossom Time', 'Melancholy Baby' and 'You Are My Sunshine'. The men would gather at one end of the hall and the women at the other, waiting to be formally asked for a dance.

On one occasion, a tall Canadian soldier approached Mary and smiled. 'You're the girl who brought our laundry,' he remarked. 'I'm Leslie. Would you care to dance?'

He was tanned, with a soothing voice and a ready smile, and Mary greatly enjoyed his company that evening. He became one of her regular dancing partners – the two young people looked out for one another every week and gravitated towards each other happily. Mary liked this feeling of having a man to care for her, and although she never had any real romantic attachment to him, Leslie's attention felt reassuring and protective.

At the end of one evening, a few weeks after they had first met, he asked her whether she fancied going to tea with him in Eastbourne that Sunday. After a moment's pause – after all, a proper date where they'd be alone was a very different proposition to dancing in public – Mary agreed. She liked him. It was flattering to be asked. How could she not go? However, when she told Pierce about the invitation he wasn't at all happy about a soldier calling for her. Soldiers didn't enjoy a good name.

'We can't have soldiers knocking at the house,' he said. 'It'll give you a bad reputation. And what will the neighbours think?'

He didn't say she couldn't go, though, and the neighbours didn't have to know. So the next time she called at the Canadians' camp on her laundry round, she asked a familiar face there to pass on the message to Leslie that she would meet him at the café in Eastbourne at one o'clock that coming Sunday.

On the day, an unusually anxious Mary wondered whether Leslie had got the message and whether he would actually be there. Or perhaps he had forgotten about it? She voiced her concerns to her father, who she found in the front room, seated in the armchair, reading his newspaper. The headline screamed that America had declared war after Japanese planes had attacked the US Pacific Fleet at Pearl Harbor, killing over 2,400 Americans in the process.

'Shouldn't be long now,' he said.

'Who shouldn't?' Mary asked, her mind on Leslie.

'The war. Shouldn't go on much longer now. We've got the Yanks on our side.' He folded his newspaper with a sense of satisfaction. 'About bloody time,' he muttered.

Mary stood watching him, clearly nervous.

'Want me to come with you?' he asked.

Mary grimaced. 'I'm not a little girl,' she replied. 'I don't know what to do.'

'Why don't we get the bus together and if you see him outside the tea shop, then you can go off alone,' said Pierce. 'But if he doesn't turn up, then we can come back together.'

Mary smiled. 'Yeah. Thanks, Dad,' she said.

To her relief, when they arrived in Eastbourne and started walking down the High Street, Mary spotted Leslie in the distance, outside the café.

'That's him,' she said to her father excitedly, and quickly kissed him goodbye.

'Don't run!' he called after her. 'It's not seemly.'

Mary slowed down and Pierce watched her for a moment longer before turning and making his way back to the bus stop. His girls were growing up fast, he thought to himself. He was trying his best as a parent but he was only with them at the weekends, and there was only so much he could do with the time he had.

Once again, his thoughts turned to Annie. He could never be their mother, he knew that. Annie had always seemed to know exactly what to say or do. He knew he'd done the right thing today, though, and felt pleased with himself.

Indeed, Mary did feel very grown up, sipping from china crockery in the tea shop, seated opposite her date at a small table draped in white linen. Leslie ordered cakes for them, which Mary thought very extravagant, but she did her best to be nonchalant and sophisticated. Casting an eye around the room, she saw other, older couples in quiet conversation and although she felt a little out of place in such fine surroundings, she was definitely enjoying the experience. She might not have been particularly attracted to Leslie, but he had good manners and was extremely attentive, with a nice line in flattery. He made her feel good.

Thanks to her mischievous sisters, things didn't go quite so well as he accompanied her back to Battle Road. As they were walking along the pavement, Mary had noticed Joan and Anne walking a little distance behind them on the other side of the street. Feeling mischievous, Joan crossed the road with Anne and stepped up the pace so that soon they were right behind Mary and Leslie. She bent down and whispered something in Anne's ear. Two-year-old Anne looked puzzled but, doing as Joan asked, ran up to Mary, tugged her on the arm and said in a loud voice, 'What have we got for tea, Mum?'

Leslie looked shocked. Mary, her face flushing, turned to see a laughing Joan. She then looked back at Leslie. 'It's not what you think!' she burst out. She explained hurriedly that her sisters were playing a prank on her and was relieved when Leslie laughed too.

One evening a week, Mary and Iris were part of the local fire-watch. They teamed up at Hailsham Senior Mixed School with two men – one in his sixties who was too old to join the armed forces and the other, at sixteen, too young. There, they would sit in a disused classroom, where there were some camp beds for them to sleep on, and whenever the air-raid siren sounded they would go up to the roof and watch for any incendiary bombs being dropped. Their job would then be to raise the alarm and to help extinguish the fire.

One night, Mary was in such a deep sleep that she didn't hear the air-raid siren sound and the others, deciding not to rouse her, made their way to the roof. However, shortly after being left alone, Mary was startled out of her sleep by a scuttling noise nearby. It was a moment or two before she was awake enough to realize that she'd been left on her own, and that the noise must be a mouse. Deciding that bombs were far less scary than a small rodent, she shot out of bed to join the others on the roof.

Despite its various perils, Mary enjoyed the job, and the extra money it brought in – 3 shillings a shift – paid for her to go to the pictures at the local cinema the following night, which she considered to be a luxury. It was something she looked forward to eagerly and her usual companion on such trips was another Bermondsey evacuee, Nellie Wallace. The pair would go all misty-eyed when their favourite film stars were on screen. Errol Flynn was always popular but, in Mary's eyes, Tyrone Power was the most handsome man she'd ever seen.

One evening, the pair of them had gone to the cinema to watch *The Hound of the Baskervilles*, starring Basil Rathbone as Sherlock Holmes and Nigel Bruce as Dr Watson. They were so spooked by the story about the legend of the supernatural hound stalking the moorland at night, that when they came out into the darkness they were too terrified to walk home alone.

'I don't fancy it at all, do you?' Mary asked her friend nervously. Nellie shook her head. Then, Mary looked over to see a man, who she half recognized, coming out of the cinema. She knew that he lived quite near her house.

'Wait here a moment,' she said to Nellie. She approached the man, turning on the charm that she used to great effect at the dances, by admitting that she and Nellie had both been scared witless by the film and asked if he would mind accompanying them home. He was happy to do so, amused by their plight, and walked them safely to their front doors.

Mary felt a little foolish afterwards. After all, they were in the middle of a war, with the real-life horror of death and bloodshed, yet here she was, in Hailsham, afraid of a movie about a hound! She wondered what her mother would have thought of her.

Mary and Leslie continued to see each other on a casual basis for a couple of months before drifting apart. It had been fun, and Mary had done a lot of growing up, but it would be another Canadian soldier who would steal her attention at the dance hall and get well and truly under her skin. Meeting him was to change her life.

CHAPTER 6

Christmas Tear

Anne (centre) is flanked by Kath (left), and Pat. Feeling pretty in the dresses Mary made for them.

IN THE RUN-UP to Christmas, back in Bermondsey, Annie would always take her daughters 'down The Blue', the term that locals used for Southwark Park Road, named after the Blue Anchor public house. The road was lined with shops and market stalls which stayed open till late; the pick 'n' mix sweet counter at Woolworths drew young children like iron filings to a magnet and the stalls outside sold a variety of goods, including linen, fruit and veg, and clothes. The children's hearts would thump with excitement as people bustled about, preparing for the upcoming celebrations, but the festive period always brought extra financial stress for Pierce and Annie.

The older girls, Mary in particular, were acutely aware that money was, in fact, in short supply all year round. One of Mary's jobs was the weekly visit to the pawnbroker, which she hated. Every Monday morning, Annie would wrap up a parcel for her to take along, which would be exchanged for a loan of a few shillings. Jewellery, ornaments, clothes and shoes were all viable and Pierce's best suit was a favourite item to pawn, as he had no occasion to wear it during the week.

Mary would dash along the street with the parcel, hoping to avoid her friends because she felt so ashamed. The following Friday evening she would be back there, clutching whatever Annie could spare, usually one or two shillings.

Once the interest was taken out of that, she would use the remainder to pay off all or part of the loan and would retrieve as many items as possible, always starting with the shoes. Next Monday she would be back again, often with the same bundle, and she'd tell the pawnbroker, 'Mummy says the same as last week, please.' This time he would hand over slightly less cash, because the goods were a week older. If the full repayment, plus interest had not been paid by the end of the month he kept the belongings – that was the rather brutal deal.

In a rare act of kindness, the aunts had made their nieces red and white spotted dresses for Easter. The children were delighted and loved them. They didn't have them for long, though, because grudgingly, a desperate Annie pawned these too, intent on getting them back but despairing when she was unable to come up with the money. Mary would never forget feeling the mixed emotions of shame, resentment and indignation when she'd seen two local girls wearing the dresses. *Their* dresses.

Living in such financial difficulty meant that every penny helped. Uncle Jack, Grandmother Kate's brother, lived opposite them on Abbey Street and every week he would visit Kate. If the girls were there too, he would give them a penny between them. It wasn't much but it was something, and Annie used to make sure that her daughters were there in order to receive the gift.

'Go downstairs to Granny's,' she would say. 'Uncle Jack's arrived.'

The girls would traipse downstairs dutifully, pretending that they were simply visiting, and wait and wait until it was time for Jack to rummage in his pocket for a penny. He always made a big show of it and Kate would sit there, tutting, because he dragged it out for so long. When the penny was eventually handed over, the girls all had to give him a kiss and would then go back upstairs. They didn't reap the reward to spend on treats, though – they secretly handed it over to Annie to put in the gas meter.

At Christmas, finding the money to buy small presents for their five children, as well as extra food and drink, was so difficult that Pierce always needed to ask a friend of his at the Electricity Board for a Christmas loan. Shrewd Annie would leave their main shopping trip until Christmas Eve, when trees and turkeys were sold off cheaply rather than not being sold at all, and in Woolworths, where everything was priced under sixpence, the girls were able to spend what little money Annie had been able to squirrel away for them. There, they bought small but heartfelt Christmas gifts for each other.

One year, just before Christmas, Pierce was delighted to be told that he was going to receive a wage rise. When he came home and told Annie the good news, she was even more excited than him.

'That's wonderful, Pierce!' she said. 'Well done. How much will it be?'

Pierce gave a little smile. 'It's not going to change our lives. I'm still going to do the pools.'

Annie gave him a wry look. 'With the amount of effort you put into that, it's about time we won something,' she said, thinking of him in the armchair each week, hunched over the coupon, trying to forecast correctly that Saturday's football match results.

'I'm told it'll bring my wage up to four pounds, though,' he added.

It wasn't much but nevertheless it would make a

difference, and Annie thought that £4 sounded a lot more impressive than £3 17s.

When the day came that he was due to receive his increased pay packet, Annie was in high spirits, proud of her husband for reaching the £4 benchmark.

'Daddy's got a rise at work, girls. He'll be bringing home extra money tonight,' she said, sharing her pride and enthusiasm with her daughters. She could barely wait for him to finish work and, as it neared the time for his arrival, she gathered her daughters around her to wait outside the house for him. The girls were a little bemused but were happy enough to wait for their father's return, as their mother became increasingly excited.

'Here he comes!' she exclaimed, as she saw Pierce in the distance, striding purposefully towards them. As they started waving, Pierce saw them and shook his fist in the air triumphantly, indicating that he had got the money. Annie kissed and hugged him warmly on the doorstep, as though he were a returning conqueror.

Before they went shopping on Christmas Eve, there used to be much excitement amongst the girls as they waited for Granddad to call them downstairs for his traditional festive routine. Over the course of the year he would have saved any new, shiny pennies that came his way and placed them in a little red money box in the shape of a pillar box, which he kept on the window ledge. The girls would gather excitedly at the top of the stairs, waiting for the call. When it came, they had to stop themselves from stampeding down and causing each other bodily harm.

In his living room, Granddad would be sitting in an armchair, smiling up at them as they jostled around him.

'Right. Who would like to pass me my money box?' he would say, and there would be a race to get it from the window ledge. Granddad would give it a good rattle and make appreciative noises as the girls beamed at him in anticipation.

'Well, now, there sounds like there is quite a bit in here,' he would tease. Then, taking a knife, which had been placed carefully on the side table next to him, he would slide it part way into the slot and tip the box. A golden penny would slide down the knife and plop out of the opening. Holding it up, between finger and thumb, he would look meaningfully at the girls.

'Oldest first,' he would announce and proffer the coin to Mary, who would step forward eagerly and hold out her hand as he dropped the penny into her palm.

Once all the girls had a coin, the procedure would be repeated until the box was empty. The girls remained wide-eyed at the sight of one shiny coin sliding out after another. If they were lucky, they might have four or five pennies each, enough for some small toys, such as a yo-yo that could be bought for a penny or a toy drum in Woolworths, just three inches in diameter and filled with sweets. If they wanted to treat themselves, then an ice-cream cone was halfpenny and an ice-cream wafer sandwich one penny.

Once home from Christmas shopping down The Blue, the excited children were put to bed early, although all of them found it hard to sleep with the anticipation of what the next day would bring. That night, Pierce would hang up some of his socks by the fireplace for the girls and, by the time Annie had finished working her magic, each one would be bulging with an orange, an apple, a handful of nuts, a little packet of sweets, a thin book and a small toy, such as miniature tin weighing scales.

On Christmas morning there were excited squeals as the girls feverishly pulled out one delight after another from the tatty socks that had been magically transformed into Christmas stockings. In truth, what the girls received was little in terms of material form but they loved and cherished everything that they were given.

Annie's parents would join the family upstairs for Christmas dinner of turkey and vegetables and a homemade apple pie. Then, in the evening, they would all go downstairs for a party with visiting aunts, uncles and cousins on Annie's side of the family. Her brothers Arthur and Tom would be there with their wives, as would Annie's Uncle Jack who lived opposite, her other brother Mike and the girls' cousin Kit. The house came alive and everyone had their own party piece, including the children. Mary and Joan always rehearsed some dance moves together and over time perfected what they called 'The Irish Fling' and 'The Sailor's Hornpipe'.

Granddad caused some sniggering amongst the girls because he would traditionally sing a song they had never heard anywhere else, which included the recurring line 'Over the burning sands of Egypt', and seemed to go on for ever! Standing with a glass of beer in his hand, he would sing verse after verse, and at frequent intervals the girls would clap enthusiastically in the hope that he was finished but each time he would take a deep breath and carry on. Kate would watch him appreciatively and shoot sharp looks at her granddaughters whenever they clapped prematurely, saying crossly, 'He's not finished yet.' When he did eventually come to the end, he would mistake the heartfelt applause of relief as encouragement, prompting him to launch into 'Danny Boy'. He would become so emotional with his rendition that by the end he would be crying his eyes out!

Boxing Day was spent at Pierce's sisters' house, where there would be another singalong with various relatives on his side of the family this time. Aunt Rose's speciality was 'Two Little Girls In Blue', while Aunt Mary tried but – truth be told – mostly failed to accompany her on the piano. The melancholy song began:

> An old man gazed on a photograph, in the locket he'd worn for years;
> His nephew then asked him the reason why that picture had cost him tears.
> 'Come listen,' he said, 'I will tell you, my lad, a story that's strange but true.
> Your father and I, at the school one day, met two little girls in blue.'

Then, the adults and the girls, all familiar with the song, would join in with the chorus:

> 'Two little girls in blue, lad, two little girls in blue.
> They were sisters, we were brothers and learned to love the two.
> And one little girl in blue, lad, who won your father's heart,
> Became your mother, I married the other, but now we have drifted apart.'

All of these happy memories came flooding back the first Christmas that Pierce and the girls spent without

Annie. After seventeen years of marriage, Pierce was a changed man following the loss of his wife. Despite the traditional husband and wife roles that typified the era, Annie had always been the tougher of the pair. She had been the driving force who had made the pennies stretch, kept up standards, run the household and made most of the decisions. Now living with his sisters during the week in London, their company helped to take his mind off his bereavement but the feeling of loss intensified, almost like a physical pain in his stomach, as the festive time got nearer and happy memories of Christmases past began to haunt him.

He yearned to be with his children and to hug them tightly, and couldn't wait to finish work for the Christmas break and get on a train to be with them in Hailsham. He hoped that they would help to ease the pain.

On Christmas Eve he did his usual rounds, collecting money from meters for the Electricity Board, but found it difficult to focus on anything other than finishing work at lunchtime and being with his family a couple of hours later. He had been shopping down The Blue a few days earlier and had bought some sweets, books and small toys for his daughters, which he had already packed into the travel bag that was waiting at home.

Kath and Pat in particular were to be very lucky girls that year because, carefully wrapped up in newspaper and also placed in his bag, were two china dollies that had been given to him by his younger brother Albert's wife. They had sat on her dresser as ornaments over the years but now, with Annie gone and Pierce doing his best to buy his girls presents, she felt that she should pass them on.

Pierce had worried about giving such beautiful gifts to

only two of his children but didn't want to deprive Kath and Pat of them. Anne was too young for such a fragile doll, he reasoned, Mary and Joan were too old for them, and he thought Sheila might be too. So Kath and Pat seemed to be best suited and he did his best, with the help of some money from his sisters, who had taken pity on him, to buy some extra little presents for his other daughters, to make up for it.

Now on his round he noticed how, despite the escalation of war, people generally continued to be of good cheer, and he was greeted with smiles and hearty hails of 'Merry Christmas' at many of the houses he called at. He managed a wan smile in return but how could he tell them that he was still in mourning? It had only been six months since Annie's death and it felt as raw as ever – even more so at such an emotional time of the year. Merry Christmas? For some, maybe, he thought.

The morning seemed to drag. He checked his watch regularly and when he was finally able to finish work, he hurried back home, packed some last-minute belongings into his bag and headed for London Bridge station with his heavy luggage in one hand and a box of fruit he had bought as a Christmas treat tucked under his other arm.

Train services were limited on Christmas Eve and he was unable to travel directly to Polegate, the nearest station to Hailsham, so he boarded one that necessitated changing trains. As he journeyed out of London, though, his mind racing with thoughts of his girls waiting for him and of Christmases past, he went flying past his station and had to alight further down the line. There was then a long wait before he could get a train back in the other direction, and an even longer wait before getting the next one to Polegate.

It was eventually dark as his train pulled in to Polegate. The station was deserted and there was no bus service to Hailsham. Everyone, it seemed, was already home for Christmas. The journey had been stressful, Pierce hadn't spoken to anyone for hours, and he was feeling lonely and depressed. He should have been with his family by now. Instead, he was still some way off – about three miles – and the pitch black of the countryside during the wartime blackout was considerably more disorientating than in London with its buildings and pavements and people. Always people. There was nothing else to do but to set off on foot and hope to hitch a lift if he saw a passing vehicle.

The cold bit through his old overcoat, his arms ached from carrying the bag and the box of fruit, and his despair increased with every step. The only thought that kept him going was his gaggle of girls, waiting to greet him in the warmth of their country kitchen.

At Battle Road, the girls waited anxiously for their father, wondering when he would arrive. It was getting later and later. Pierce's sisters, too, were concerned about his whereabouts.

'Is Daddy *ever* coming?' asked Pat.

'He probably had to work later than he thought,' Joan answered. 'I'm sure he'll be here soon.' But she knew he should have been with them hours ago. Already missing their mother, Joan was struggling to keep her sisters' spirits up in Pierce's absence.

For Pierce, the walk seemed to go on for ever and there were times when he worried that he'd taken the wrong turning – all the signposts and place names had been removed, in case the Germans invaded. He could hardly see anything in front of him and no vehicles had passed by.

Christmas Tear

Every now and then he had to stop and put the bag and box down to rest his arms. The fresh fruit had seemed a lovely idea at the time. Now he regretted bringing it.

After almost an hour, he began seriously to wonder whether he was going in the right direction. Just when he became completely exasperated, convinced he simply wasn't going to make it, he heard a noise behind him. It was the sound of an engine. He turned and saw the dipped lights of a vehicle in the distance. As it approached, Pierce put down his bag and stuck out his thumb in a hitchhiking gesture. He felt a burst of hope as the car stopped and a man's head emerged from the window.

'Where are you going?' asked the driver.

'Battle Road,' Pierce replied.

'You're in luck. Get in and we'll drop you off.'

Pierce breathed a huge sigh of relief. The man got out to help him put his belongings in the boot, and Pierce jumped into the back seat, next to an even bigger brown cardboard box than his own. The woman in the front passenger seat turned and smiled at him.

'Sorry about the squeeze,' she said, and explained that they had just been to a party and were bringing home some of the balloons and other party decorations.

'Oh, I'm just so relieved to get a lift,' Pierce replied. 'I've had the most horrendous journey.'

Pierce told them of his travels and said he was going to see his daughters. During their conversation, it transpired that the couple knew Mary because she collected and delivered their laundry. As the couple listened sympathetically, Pierce's pain and anxiety poured out when he talked about the loss of his beloved Annie and how it would be the girls' first Christmas without their mother.

When they pulled up outside the house in Battle Road, Pierce couldn't thank them enough. It was their pleasure, the kind couple told him. But his emotional state hadn't gone unnoticed. As Pierce stepped out of the car, the man, on a whim, picked up the cardboard box from the back seat.

'Here, take this,' he said.

'I can't take that,' Pierce replied.

'Yes, you can. I can't think of a better home for it. Anyway, it's not for you. It's for your girls; for them to decorate the house with.'

The man carried the box down the path to the side door and Pierce shook his hand warmly and thanked him for his kindness once more. He stood to watch the car drive off down the road, waving them goodbye, then he heard the sound he had longed to hear for what seemed like an age.

'Daddy!' The door was flung open and the girls rushed to him, hugging him and dragging him inside. Pierce felt a lump in his throat and tried to fight back the tears welling in his eyes, but it was no good. He was so overcome with emotion at being reunited finally with his girls that his eyes began to water. Unable to contain himself any longer, he burst into tears.

The girls were shocked. 'What is it, Daddy?' they chorused. 'What's wrong?'

Embarrassed, Pierce shook his head and spluttered, 'I'm just so happy to see you. That's all.'

Nell looked at him and softened. She had little compassion for others but Pierce was her brother and she loved him. She squeezed his hand gently, reassuringly.

'Sit down,' she told him. 'You're here now.' However,

Pierce just couldn't control the tears that coursed down his cheeks.

'Fruit!' exclaimed Kath, as she noticed the box of apples, pears and nuts on the floor.

'What's in this other one, Daddy?' asked Pat, her hands already on the box that had so generously been donated.

'Hush now,' said Nell. 'Let your dad rest for a while.'

The girls could barely contain themselves but, once Pierce had recuperated with a double dose of family warmth and a glass of beer, he helped his delighted daughters pull out the party decorations, which they put up around the house excitedly.

'You girls need to be off to bed,' said Nell after a while. There were moans from Sheila, Kath and Pat but when Pierce reminded them that they had to be asleep before Father Christmas arrived, their spirits soared again and they took themselves off hurriedly.

After Mary and Joan had also retired for the night, Pierce became melancholic once more as, for the first time in his life, it now fell to him to cram his socks with little presents for the girls. Although his sisters helped him out, he missed his wife dearly. There was an absence of fun and he longed for her to be there; to hear her voice, feel her presence, share a laugh and to hold her in his arms.

Pierce sat chatting with his sisters for another hour, over one more beer and a cigarette, which helped to lighten his mood. Then, when he judged that the girls were asleep, he crept as quietly as he could up the steep staircase, past the precariously placed toilet, carrying his gift-laden socks, and put his ear to one of the bedroom doors, listening for any sound. All he could hear was sleepy breathing and light snoring, so he crept in and gently placed a sock at the foot of each bed, smiling softly at Sheila, Kath, Pat and Anne's angelic faces. He exited and returned a few minutes later to sit the two china dollies carefully on top of the chest of drawers.

Back downstairs, he entered the large bedroom to the rear of the house and placed a festive sock at the end of the beds where Mary and Joan were asleep, and then got ready to retire for the night. It had been a long day and he fell asleep quickly on the downstairs sofa under a comforting blanket.

Kath awoke early in the morning. The chinks of subdued light between the curtains suggested that the darkness of night had not yet faded and the sun was yet to rise. Through her half-opened, bleary eyes, she could make out two shapes on the chest of drawers. Curious to see what they were, she opened her eyes wider and was startled to realize that the shapes were in fact two beautiful dollies. Kath felt the excitement coursing through her body but, fearing that she would ruin the magic if she got out of bed too early – and perhaps saw Father Christmas – she squeezed her eyes shut again and, with a little smile on her face, eventually went back to sleep.

Later that morning, still bright and early, there were squeals of delight when the girls woke and saw their presents. Kath and Pat in particular could scarcely believe that they had been given the dollies about which they could only dream. Neither had owned a doll before but had improvised in imaginative ways. During the summer months, they would collect flowers that had fallen from the fuchsia bush in the garden – sometimes even plucking them gently from the plant itself if Annie wasn't watching – and, holding them delicately between two fingers, bob them up and down, imagining they were pretty little ballerinas in pink tutus. They would also line them up along the top of the wall so that, in a little girl's imagination, they resembled the 'Dance of the Little Swans' from *Swan Lake*.

Even a statue of Our Lady in the bedroom would be utilized as a doll when a mother or older figure was called for!

Pierce explained quietly to his other daughters that the china dollies had in fact been given to him and that was the only reason why their younger sisters had such lavish presents. He was relieved when Mary, Joan and Sheila took it in good grace and didn't resent it at all. He was also amused to watch Kath and Pat playing with the dolls so sweetly and gently, despite being the most tomboyish of the sisters.

'Get yourself ready for church, girls,' said Aunt Rose. 'You don't want to be late. There will be a lot of people there today.' She was right. The girls managed to squeeze into one of the pews but little St Wilfrid's Church was so packed that some latecomers had to stand at the back. A church service was always torture for the girls, but today of all days they simply couldn't wait for it to end so that they could rush back home to play with their presents once more.

There was a special treat of some chicken and vegetables for Christmas dinner. Not a lot, but enough to go around. As they sat tightly packed around the kitchen table, Pierce raised his glass in the air. The excitable chatter died down gradually as, one by one, they all became aware of his posture. When all was quiet he said simply, 'To Mum.'

As his daughters and sisters raised their glasses and each took a large gulp, there was a moment of sadness before Pierce, regaining his spirit quickly, smiled and said, 'Come on then, eat up. Mum wouldn't want your food to get cold.'

In the afternoon, Kath and Pat were sitting on the floor, engrossed in playing with their dollies, when Pierce suggested the family go for a walk to 'help the food go down'.

'Come on, you two,' he encouraged. 'You can take your dollies with you, if you like.'

'No, I'll leave her here,' said Kath, after a moment's hesitation.

'I want to take mine,' said Pat.

'You can both take them,' said Pierce. 'Besides, I want people to see what lovely presents you have.'

While Pat was happy with that idea, Kath was decidedly less so. As overjoyed as she was with her present, she felt that at the age of nine she might be considered a little too old to be playing with dollies. Happily playing with it in private was one thing but in public . . . She was embarrassed by the thought of her friends seeing her. Worst still, her enemies.

'What if I drop her?' she said to her father.

'You won't. I've been watching how careful you both are. Come on. Let's show them off,' he said, thinking how delighted Annie would have been at their neighbours seeing what fine presents they could afford.

Kath reluctantly did as her father asked but, for the duration of the walk, she held the doll close to her, its face against her chest, doing her best to conceal it. She couldn't wait to get back home where she could play with it without any inhibitions. Spending as much time away from his daughters as he did, Pierce lacked the understanding that Annie would have had about her girls growing up fast and being a bit embarrassed about certain things.

That Christmas was as difficult for the girls as it was for Pierce, who, more than ever, felt the absence of Annie so keenly. Although she was in everyone's thoughts, after the toast nobody mentioned her again because they feared that it would be too painful. For the last six months, Pierce had done his best to keep strong for the girls. However, the memory of seeing their father crying uncontrollably on Christmas Eve, his emotions having got the better of him, would never be forgotten.

The new year got underway with no sign of the war ending. Pierce and his sisters continued to visit Hailsham at the weekends once the festive period was over, but the girls were becoming increasingly self-sufficient and able to look after themselves.

A visit from their aunts, always something to endure, was made even more unpleasant if the women were in a bad mood when they arrived because their free-ride scam had failed. Their scheme involved boarding the train in London, without having bought a ticket, then, on arrival in Polegate, they would alight and hide inside the platform toilets while the station attendant checked passengers' tickets. After a while he would move off and, when the coast was clear, the aunts would sneak out of the toilets and make their way quickly to the bus stop. However, having caught them once, the attendant had grown wise to their habit and had started to wait for them to emerge from the toilets so that he could ask for their tickets. To his surprise, the women would act affronted rather than abashed when confronted.

'You should get a proper job!' they would say. 'Haven't you got anything better to do with yourself?'

Pierce would stand in the background, embarrassed. His sisters had persuaded him that they could all get away with travelling for free and, after they had been proven right on the first few occasions, he had warmed more and more to the scam. He was always short of money, after all. The increasingly furtive behaviour it entailed was making him think again, though. It wasn't something that a man of his age – and a father too – should be doing. What would his daughters think? His sisters' bullish reaction to getting caught also made him wince. He loved them dearly, but there were times when he could see things from his daughters' point of view.

Meanwhile, Kath and Pat were getting into a few scrapes of their own. Fortunately for them, Joan didn't know about most of them. She did her best and tried to emulate her mother, reprimanding her younger sisters if they were naughty and administering the occasional smack, if required. If word had reached the welfare officer that a couple of young 'thieves' were living in the house, however, then Pierce would have received a stern letter saying the arrangement allowing his daughters to live without parental or adult supervision during the week was not working.

On one occasion, Kath and Pat were playing on the embankment by the railway with their friends, Cheryl Cartwright and her younger sister Iris, when they caught sight of some plump damsons on the branches of some trees overhanging a fence. Unable to resist, they picked and ate some.

'Do they belong to anyone?' asked Pat, as she bit into the juicy fruit.

'Well, they won't miss a few on this side,' said Kath. 'Besides, they're windfalls.'

'What's that?' asked Pat.

'Fruit that's fallen to the ground and will only be eaten by the birds if no one else has them.'

Pat was puzzled. 'But they're not on the ground.'

Kath looked at her sister. 'Not yet, but they're about to fall at any moment,' she replied. 'So it's silly to let them rot.'

To emphasize the point, Kath twisted one of the damsons until it came away from the branch.

'See?' she asked. 'Loose.'

This was evidence enough for Pat. She climbed up to the roof of a dilapidated-looking shed nearby so that she could reach the higher branches but, with a cracking sound, she fell through the thin, rotten wood. Groaning, she managed to pull herself out but the noise had drawn attention and they panicked when they saw a man approaching.

'Run for it!' Kath said. The girls needed no further prompting as they clambered up the embankment back towards the field. Pat hobbled along, in considerable pain, but they didn't stop running until they reached Cheryl and Iris' house.

Mrs Cartwright was alarmed by the excited, breathless jabbering of the girls as they burst through the door, and by Pat's bloody leg, which had gone unnoticed in the commotion. Pat hadn't noticed the large splinter of wood buried in her shin either and howled with pain as Mrs Cartwright pulled it out with tweezers. It was even more painful when she dabbed the wound with iodine lotion.

'Ow! What's that?' Pat cried through watery eyes.

'Just something to clean it up so that it doesn't get infected,' said Mrs Cartwright.

'It hurts like hell!' Pat complained.

'Stop making a fuss, Pat,' said Kath, feeling a little queasy as she looked at the wound.

The girls told Mrs Cartwright that they had been playing and climbing but felt it best not to mention picking the damsons. They omitted this part of the story when they got home, too, during Joan's questioning.

Pat's leg continued to play up over the next few weeks but her attention, along with her sisters', was soon distracted by something much more pleasing. One Saturday afternoon, the girls were playing in the garden when they heard, and then saw, a trail of lorries and trucks arriving in the field beyond.

'What do you think's going on, Kath?' asked Pat. As they screwed up their eyes to try to see more clearly, they could make out a colourful livery on the sides of the vehicles.

'It's a fair!' Kath shouted.

The girls ran inside to tell everyone, and Joan agreed that they could go over to the field to watch the proceedings more closely.

'Wait for me,' called Sheila, who had been lying on her bed reading a book when she heard the commotion.

Over by the field they were joined by several other eager-faced children, peering over the hedge as the vehicles and attractions trundled into place. Their excitement increased when they saw a carousel full of ornately painted carved horses and the Big Wheel arrive. The Jarman girls stood watching, transfixed by the activity, until Joan arrived to reprimand them for being late home for tea.

Christmas Tear

That evening, as they lay in their beds, they could hear the fairground workers still about their business. Usually night time was very quiet and so to listen to the sounds of hammers at work on something that would create so much pleasure was joyful to their ears.

The Jarman girls had never been to a fair before but they had experienced a taste of the gaiety it could bring via the street entertainers who sometimes visited Abbey Street. There was a horse-drawn merry-go-round, which was a penny a ride; the game of 'catch the rat', where a stuffed sock was dropped down a length of drainpipe and you had to try to trap it with a stick as it emerged at the other end; and a barrow full of buckets of goldfish, where unwanted rags could be exchanged for a fish – so long as you provided your own jam jar to take it away in.

Men, garishly made up as women, toured the street with a barrel organ. One would turn the handle to play the tinkling music and others would dance along, hitching up their heavy skirts to the amusement of the audience. There were also jugglers, magicians and a man who made the girls squeal with laughter when he chased after any passing cyclist, trying to tickle them with a feather duster.

The girls would sit on the kerb outside their house, gleefully observing the silly antics, and when the entertainers moved on to another street, they'd follow them and sit down to watch them all over again. The girls missed such delights living in Hailsham but the arrival of the fair made their spirits soar and they looked forward eagerly to the day of its opening.

All of the sisters, including Joan and Mary, went to the fair. Joan gave the younger ones the few pennies she could spare so that they could enjoy themselves on the prized

181

rides – the carousel, the Big Wheel and the Big Dipper. Even when they had no money to spend, while the fair was there they would head over most days to enjoy the sights, sounds and confectionery smells. In the early evening, as the younger ones settled into bed, they could hear the faint music of the carousel playing popular songs, such as 'Don't Fence Me In' by Cole Porter, and would fall asleep with a gentle smile on their faces.

It was during this summer of 1942 that Mary got talking to a local girl named Barbara at a dance at Magham Down. They took a liking to each other and Barbara told Mary that she was in the Land Army, working on a farm in Battle Road. With German U-boats continuing to target merchant ships bringing food supplies into Britain, the Women's Land Army played a vital role in helping to increase the production of home-grown produce in order to keep the nation fed. Mary had seen the government posters and newspaper adverts extolling the virtues of enrolling. She was particularly struck by the poster depicting a Land Army girl, pitchfork in hand, standing in a field bathed in sunshine beneath the slogan, 'For a healthy, happy job join the Women's Land Army'.

The Government paid farmers to employ Land Army girls and that money was used to pay the girls' wages. Mary was intrigued and liked the idea of working so close to home. She asked Barbara all about it.

'Oh, it's lovely,' said Barbara. 'Out in the fresh air. Lots of sunshine. It's not really like work at all and it's respected because it's making an important contribution to the war effort. Plus, you get a smart uniform to wear. It's a good job with decent pay and a lot of variety. I can put a word in for you, if you like. The farmer, Mr Burton, is looking for another girl to drive the milk van. You could do that. It'd be fun. We'd be working together.'

Mary liked driving the laundry delivery van but it had begun to feel a little repetitive. The sheen had worn off and she found herself swept up by the idea of working on the farm. The Land Army pay was better too, according to Barbara. It all seemed to be positive, with no negatives that she could see. Mary knew she would need to talk it over with Pierce, though, and she told Barbara she would do so over the weekend.

Pierce was hunched over a shoe last in the kitchen when Mary approached him. Whenever the girls' shoes needed mending he would bring the last down with him from Bermondsey, along with strips of leather and nails. The girls would often sit and watch him at work, marvelling at his expertise but apprehensive that he might swallow one of the nails held between his lips. If a hole appeared in one of their shoes when Pierce wasn't there with his repair kit, the girls would take the temporary measure of cutting a sole from cardboard, which they would then insert inside the shoe until he could fix it properly the following weekend.

'If that's what you want to do then it's OK with me,' he said, looking up at Mary from the last. 'But I don't want you moving away from Hailsham,' he added. 'You've got to be here for each other.'

Mary beamed and assured him that she didn't want to work anywhere other than at the Battle Road farm, anyhow. The proximity to home was a large part of the job's attraction as it would mean more take-home pay in her pocket each week. Many Land Army girls worked a long way from home and had to live on the farm, paying the farmer out of their wages for their accommodation.

Barbara arranged for Mary to meet Mr Burton one day after work. A short, stocky man, Mary thought him rather blunt in his manner but imagined that was what all farmers were like.

'I expect they're more used to dealing with animals than people,' she said to Joan that evening as they enjoyed a cup of cocoa before going to bed.

Mr Burton wrote a letter for Mary to take to the local Land Army offices in Lewes, stating that he needed another girl to work on his farm and that he considered Mary to be perfectly suitable. Mary then took the day off work and caught the bus into Lewes. At the Land Army offices, she sat nervously while being interviewed by a panel of two men and a woman who, amongst other things, asked her about her general health, any previous jobs she had done and her two desired locations for working. Mary then showed them the letter from Mr Burton. After a little quiet discussion between the members of the panel, the man who was seated in the middle looked over and smiled at Mary.

'Well, you have good driving experience, you're local and seem to be in good health and, if Mr Burton would like you, we have no objection,' he said.

Mary looked at him for a moment. 'So . . . Does that mean . . . ?' she began.

'It means yes,' he interjected. 'We'd be happy to have you in the Land Army, working with Mr Burton.'

An excited Mary returned home to tell everyone the good news and Barbara was delighted. Mr Burton said that as a final requirement she would need to provide him with a job reference from her current employer, which was where Mary encountered an unexpected problem. Mr Leslie, her manager at Silverlight Laundry, was not happy when she informed him that she was leaving, and tried his best to stop her.

'You're exempt from the Forces because you're already helping the war effort with us – cleaning the army camps' uniforms,' he said.

Mary remained firm, saying that the Land Army had accepted her, that she was keen to work outside and have a change of scene, and was going whether he liked it or not. He finally came to terms with her decision when she agreed to teach Iris how to drive the delivery van so that she could take on Mary's job.

He wrote the reference for her to take to Mr Burton and it was glowing – Mary had done a fine job. However, it also included the word 'stubborn', followed by a pointed exclamation mark, leaving her new employer in no doubt as to Mary's character.

After filling out the required paperwork for enrolment, Mary was issued with her Land Army uniform – a dark green jersey, brown corduroy breeches and a wide leather belt, a cream short-sleeved top with an open necked collar, khaki knee-length socks, brown shoes, a brown coat and a matching felt hat.

Once back home, she couldn't wait to try the clothes on and was thrilled with her new look. It made a welcome change from the threadbare dresses she was used to and she thought how proud her mum would have been if she could see her at that moment.

On her very first day at work, Mary realized she had made an awful mistake. For one thing, she was frightened of cows and was going to have to spend a lot of time dealing with them. Mr Burton was indeed a brusque, no-nonsense type and had no time for Mary's concern when she admitted to him that she didn't like being near the animals.

'Well, that's of no use to me,' he said. 'You'll have to get used to them. Besides, there's nothing to be frightened of. They're more scared of you than you are them.'

Mary sincerely doubted this.

'Here, take this stick. When I herd the cows from that field into this one,' he said, pointing into the distance, 'you stand by the gate and make sure they all go through.'

Mary looked at him with some alarm. 'But what if they don't want to?' she asked.

'That's what the stick's for,' he replied.

Reluctantly, Mary traipsed over to the gate, her feet sticking in the mud. As the cows headed her way, she became terrified. She stood well back from them, knowing that she would never be able to persuade any of them to go through the gate if they didn't want to! Fortunately, she had little to do, as the cows appeared to be pretty well rehearsed in this particular manoeuvre.

Mr Burton was also a censorious and religious man for whom the idea of any form of fun or enjoyment was frowned upon, as Mary discovered later that day when she was given the job of washing the used milk bottles. As she stood by the large sink, she began to whistle a cheerful tune. As soon as her new employer heard her, he bristled.

'I don't want you whistling!' he barked from the doorway, making her jump. 'A whistling woman and a crowing hen are neither fit for God nor men.'

Mary was shocked. It was only midday and she was already yearning to be back in her nice, clean laundry van, on the road and chatting with Iris. Instead, she was waddling knee-deep in mud and breathing not the fresh air that Barbara, as well as those glowing posters, had promised, but the overwhelming stench of cow dung! The thought of what she had given up for this, and of knowing that there was no way back, made her tearful. The last time she'd made a mistake like this, Annie had sorted it out for her. This time she was on her own.

During her next break she had some heated words for Barbara for painting such a rosy picture of the job. And why hadn't she mentioned how difficult Mr Burton was to work with?

'He's OK, once you get to know him,' Barbara replied defensively. Mary wasn't convinced. Finally, a sheepish Barbara admitted what she'd done. 'I just wanted the company of another girl,' she confessed.

Some time had passed since Mary had needed someone else to sort out her problems, and her newfound resilience in getting on with things, come what may, shone through. Putting her best foot forward, she welcomed the £2 wages at the end of each week, knowing how much she deserved it.

With time, she began to use her natural creativity and guile to find ways of making the job bearable. She hated cleaning the cow stalls after milking – the smell made her feel sick. Sometimes, she'd only just finished cleaning up the mess when one of the cows let nature take its course and, once again, with a resigned sigh, she would have to reach for the shovel, the broom and a bucket of water. So, after a while Mary devised a way of preventing the cows from messing up their shed when she had barely finished cleaning it. If she saw a cow lift up its tail, she would quickly grab said tail and hold it down to prevent the animal from defecating. This meant the urge would temporarily go away, giving Mary time to finish and get out. It would then be down to Iris to clean up any subsequent mess when it was her turn in the cow stalls. It was only many years later that Mary was to think about the possibility that this might have been quite uncomfortable for the cows.

In reality, Mary never actually got to drive the milk van but she would accompany Mr Burton, sitting on the open back, perched on a milk crate. When they set off on their first outing together, Mary was tense with apprehension. She could feel herself wobbling amidst the clinking milk bottles in their crates. Then, disaster struck as he drove over a bump and Mary, along with the crate, toppled into the road.

She sat on the cold ground, wincing, as she watched the van continue on its way, Mr Burton oblivious to what had happened. He was some distance down the road before he realized Mary was no longer with him and headed back. Getting out of the van, he walked over, looked down at her and, to her astonishment, asked, 'Have you broken any of the bottles?'

Pierce's optimism about the war ending soon, now 'the Yanks' had joined, was dulled as the conflict see-sawed between Allied and Axis successes. American and Filipino forces had surrendered at Bataan on 9 April 1942 and the Philippines fell to Japan. Two months later, General Rommel's Panzer division routed the British–Allied garrison at Tobruk, Libya, forcing them to retreat. Churchill called the defeat 'a disgrace'. It all made for depressing and worrying reading in the newspapers.

Christmas Tear

Pierce folded up his *News of the World* as he sat at a table in the George Inn in Hailsham, took a large gulp of beer and sighed. More bad news was to come. In the middle of August, more than 6,000 predominantly Canadian soldiers attempted to seize the German-occupied French port of Dieppe but suffered heavy casualties and were forced into a humiliating retreat just six hours later.

As the autumn leaves began to fall and the first frosts of winter started to set in, nobody was expecting the coming Christmas to be a peaceful one. However, there was to be a turnaround on the war front that lifted the British people's spirits. Throughout September and October, General Montgomery, that master of manoeuvre, had put in motion a plan to overwhelm the Germans at El Alamein, North Africa, with an influx of troops, tanks and artillery guns. It resulted in Allied forces breaking through enemy lines at the end of October, with Germany in full retreat on 4 November. After a bad run it was the victory that Churchill desperately needed.

CHAPTER 7

Dancing and Romancing

Aunt Nell and Aunt Rose with Joan (left) and Mary.

A LOCAL BOY named Ron Hoodwin, whose parents owned a farm, took a shine to Mary. In return, she thought he and his older brother, Geoff, quite handsome. When she saw Ron walking towards her along the High Street one Sunday afternoon, she noticed that he was looking straight at her. They exchanged small, shy smiles and had almost passed each other when she heard him speak.

'Would you . . . Would you like to go out sometime?' he asked haltingly. Mary turned to face him. 'Pictures, dance or . . . anywhere you like,' he added.

Mary was flattered but it took only a moment or two for her to reply, 'I don't really want to go out with anyone in particular right now. But thanks, anyway.'

Ron nodded in acceptance and continued on his walk.

'Why didn't you say yes?' Joan asked Mary when she told her about it at home. 'He's really good looking. So's his brother.'

Mary shrugged. 'I prefer the Canadians to the local boys,' she said. She didn't know it yet but one soldier in particular was about to attract her attention.

In the winter of 1942, Mary, now eighteen, arrived at the Drill Hall with her friend Iris Packham. A dance was taking place there but they'd barely got through the door before a Canadian soldier approached Mary and drawled, 'Can I have this dance, Red?'

She was taken aback by his cheeky remark and replied, 'When I take my coat off.'

Mary exchanged an amused glance with Iris as they handed their coats to the cloakroom attendant.

The soldier introduced himself as Frank Marshall. He was swarthy and dapper, with a thin moustache of the type sported by Errol Flynn. Mary liked the look of him but things got off to a rocky start when they took to the dance floor.

'Are you Italian?' Mary asked. Frank took this as an insult.

'Christ, no!' he spluttered, appalled by Mussolini's pandering to Hitler and the Italian hostility against British troops in Africa. 'I'd sooner you ask me if I'm German than Italian!'

However, things warmed up and he told her that he was from Calgary, Alberta, but had been born in England, in the northeast city of Durham.

Mary found Frank easy to talk to and he made her laugh with his seemingly endless supply of jokes – and Mary had always enjoyed laughter, even when it was at her own expense. After the dance he walked her home. As usual, as they approached the house Mary could see her father outside, throwing a cigarette onto the pavement and treading on it before going back inside. He was often to be found smoking out front, but Mary suspected he was also keeping an eye out for her.

As she said goodnight to Frank, he asked if he might see her again.

'I expect you'll see me at the next dance, if you're there,' she said, smiling. Frank nodded.

'I'll be there,' he said, and they held each other's gaze

for a moment or two before he turned and walked away. Mary watched him for a while before closing the door. She smiled to herself.

'Who was that?' Pierce asked her as she walked into the kitchen.

'Just one of the Canadians,' she replied breezily. 'We had a few dances together and he was walking back this way.'

Pierce looked at her for a while. 'You're a bit late,' he said pointedly. Mary was no later than usual, but she had learnt that it was best to say nothing whenever Pierce made this customary remark after she returned home from dancing. It would only lead to further questioning and accusations. He cared about her, and she knew he was just looking out for her, so instead, she just kissed him goodnight and took herself off to bed.

It was some time before she fell asleep that night. Her thoughts kept returning to the dance and to Frank, and she felt herself smiling even as she finally dozed off.

The following weekend couldn't come soon enough for her, and when she walked in to the Drill Hall with Iris and saw Frank watching her, she turned and hid a smile as he promptly made his way over.

'Like a dance, Mary?' he asked.

'Well, at least I've taken my coat off this time,' she replied.

Frank made sure that no one else got to dance with her that evening. He wasn't the best dance partner she'd ever had. He could manage the slow numbers all right, but was quite clumsy when it came to anything upbeat. Yet she enjoyed every moment in his company, and the feeling was clearly mutual. He also made sure that no one else got to dance with her in the weeks that followed either and slowly a romance developed. As well as the dances, they would go for walks in the rec together and occasionally to the cinema. It was six weeks before Frank kissed her and their embrace left her with a warm glow and a heady sensation. So this was what love felt like, she thought to herself.

Mary didn't invite Frank into the house during the early days of their romance but after they'd been seeing each other for a while she told Pierce about him. Not for the first time, Pierce wished Annie was around to say the right thing. He was anxious about his eldest daughter's growing interest in men but found it difficult and embarrassing to engage in what he felt should be a traditional mother–daughter conversation. In particular, he worried about his daughter getting too involved with a soldier who could be moved off anywhere with his regiment at a moment's notice.

The Jarmans' next-door neighbour, Mrs Goldsmith, whom the girls had come to call Nursey Goldsmith, was attentive to the comings and goings at the house. When observation was not sufficient she craftily questioned young Anne, who was too innocent to sense that she was being nosy. Having noticed Frank's regular visits, one day Nursey leant over the garden fence to ask Anne, who was playing in the garden on her own, 'Does that soldier stay at your place?'

Anne said that he didn't, so Mary's reputation in Battle Road remained intact, but Mary was furious when Anne later told her what Nursey Goldsmith had asked.

'Bloomin' nosy parker!' she exclaimed indignantly.

There was no stopping their neighbour's inquisitive nature, though, and in another incident, not long after,

Anne's response to questioning left Nursey Goldsmith speechless.

Mary had strained her back trying to move a full milk churn on the farm, and the doctor told her she needed to take a week's rest.

'I'm going to be under the doctor for a while,' she told her sisters, secretly welcoming the opportunity to relax at home. When Nursey asked Anne why her sister wasn't at work, she was startled by the reply, 'She's underneath the doctor!'

German planes were still flying over the south coast of England and there was a sharp reminder of just how dangerous it could be, living in Hailsham, after one unusual incident in February 1943.

A German bomb in Hailsham town centre caused an extraordinary chain of events which had people fleeing for cover. The aircraft flew in low over the rec, then dropped its bomb, which fell on the post office in George Street. The missile didn't go off immediately but instead bounced along the ground, damaging the sorting office, telephone exchange and fire station, before trundling along to the church where it came to a halt and detonated. The windows of the church and many of the nearby shops were blown out by the explosion and there was the loss of one life. The incident shook everyone living in Hailsham and made them even more apprehensive when German planes flew over.

Another of Mary's friends, Nora Collins, had started to date a Canadian soldier in the same regiment as Frank. However, in the early days of their courtship she didn't want her parents to know about him, so she arranged with Mary that she would meet the soldier at the Jarmans' house in Battle Road. The Jarman girls were puzzled by this new young man – in particular his lack of social graces. He would come into their home, sit down and not say a word to anyone. This continued until he arrived one Saturday evening when Pierce was down from London. Walking in, the soldier took a seat as usual without saying a word. When Pierce came downstairs, he was surprised to find a stranger sitting in his favourite armchair.

They exchanged glances but, in his usual fashion, the soldier said nothing. Pierce was so perplexed that he couldn't think of anything to say either. He stood for a moment, staring at the soldier, then walked out to the kitchen where he found Mary washing some dishes.

'Something funny just happened,' he said, frowning.

'What's that?' asked Mary.

'Some bloke is sitting in my armchair and hasn't said a word. A Canadian soldier.' Pierce stared at Mary. 'Who the bloody hell is he?'

'Oh, he's waiting for Nora,' said Mary easily.

'Well, why doesn't he go round to her house?' Pierce asked.

Mary explained the arrangement and Pierce shook his head. 'Oh, no, he isn't. Not any more. You can't have soldiers coming and going at the house. Word will get around,' he said, thinking of the neighbours who were already twitching their lace curtains. 'I'm not having you get a reputation. And we don't want the younger ones being taken away to be looked after by someone else.'

Mary was horrified at this thought and quickly reassured her father that she would put an end to it.

'I'll sort it,' said Pierce. He went back into the front room and, as politely as he could, explained to the young man that he did not want him waiting at the house any more. If he wanted to see Nora, he would have to go to her house or meet her somewhere else.

When he was through, there was a moment's pause before the soldier got up calmly and, to Pierce's surprise, walked out, still without saying a word.

While the dances and soldiers were a great source of excitement for Mary and other girls of her age, Joan felt a certain resentment at being stuck at home day and night, weighed down with the pressure and responsibility of 'being mum' and the daily chores it involved.

She was now dropping off Anne every day at the nursery part of the school that Kath and Pat attended. There, all the toddlers would play a few games in the morning and then sleep on camp beds in the hall in the afternoon. Nursey Goldsmith had also kindly offered to have Anne for an hour or two after nursery. At her house, she would give Anne cake and a drink, and had even bought some little rag dollies for her to play with. Anne looked forward eagerly to her time spent with Nursey, and Joan appreciated her neighbour's help and generosity.

Annie had been proved right after all, when she had told her girls that Mrs Goldsmith seemed kind, despite her telling them off for stealing her loganberries.

In quiet moments at home, with Mary at work and her younger sisters at school and nursery, Joan would feel depressed. Circumstances had forced her to grow up too quickly and since Annie's death she had been missing out on the joy of youth. That was to change a little, though, when at sixteen she too started going to the dances – causing Pierce double the worry.

Pierce told Joan and Mary that if they both wanted to go to a midweek dance, they couldn't go at the same time because of the younger girls at home. So, they came to an arrangement. Joan would go for the first half of the evening, then return home so that Mary could go for the remainder.

They would often get a lift back home, along with some of the other young women, in one of the army jeeps or lorries, and at weekends Pierce wouldn't be able to relax properly until both of his older daughters were home safely. He wasn't keen on them getting into jeeps with soldiers but he didn't want them to walk home alone either. Both options caused him to worry.

He would often pick up a photograph of Annie from the mantelpiece, which showed her pushing Mary and Joan in a pram on the seafront, alongside himself, and wish with all his heart that she could pass on her advice. Annie had always known what to do. Even when she was wrong!

On Saturday nights, he would wait restlessly, straining to hear the sound of Mary and Joan's return. Even if they were just a few minutes later than expected, his anxiety would increase so much that he would have to go outside and lean on the garden gate, smoking a cigarette apprehensively, peering down the street, hoping to see them coming. The girls became used to seeing him there when they arrived home and were never convinced by his nonchalance and casual remark of 'Just having a cigarette'.

The Hoodwin brothers proved to be doubly unlucky in love when it came to the Jarman sisters. When Geoff Hoodwin asked Joan on a date, she was flattered and excited but found herself declining politely, explaining – as Mary had done with Ron – that she didn't want to date anyone for the time being. Joan surprised herself with her decision. It had been a chance to have some romance and excitement in her life but in the back of her mind was the thought that if Ron was considered to be not good enough for Mary, then it followed that Geoff was not good enough for her! Besides, Mary was right. The Canadians were more glamorous. Indeed, shortly after rejecting Geoff, she started dating an eighteen-year-old Canadian soldier named Bob Wall, who was billeted a few miles away in Eastbourne.

She had met him at a dance when he had asked her to be his partner for one of the slower numbers and, although she thought his dancing left much to be desired, she had warmed to him and thought him good looking. She also liked his ginger hair – she knew they made a striking couple. They had a couple more dances that first evening and, when the band eventually stopped playing, he asked if he could walk her home.

'But you're not going my way,' said Joan.

'I'd like to,' replied Bob, smiling.

'You'll miss your lift to Eastbourne. You can't walk back. It's nearly nine miles.'

Bob laughed. 'Why don't you let me worry about that?'

As the two of them neared the house in Battle Road, Joan became apprehensive when she saw her father leaning on the gate, smoking. Worried about what he would think of seeing her alone with a soldier, she turned to Bob and said, 'That's my dad ahead. I'm fine now. Thank you for walking me home.'

Bob asked if he might dance with her again and Joan quickly agreed before hurriedly walking the remaining few yards to her house alone.

'Had a nice evening?' asked Pierce.

'Yes. Lovely,' said Joan.

'Who was that who walked you home?'

'Bob,' said Joan, heading inside.

'Bob?'

'One of the Canadians.'

Another daughter with a soldier, Pierce thought gloomily as he followed her inside. Their hearts will surely be broken once the young men either move on or return home.

However, it was Joan who did the 'moving on' from Bob after he had walked her home regularly for a few weeks, leaving her without so much as a goodnight peck on the cheek. Indeed, all of the Canadian soldiers were very courteous and respectful towards the local girls and didn't rush things. Pierce's misgivings were entirely misplaced.

Before long, Joan started seeing another Canadian soldier named Al Hudson. He too was charming and considerate, and after they'd been going out together for a while, she even allowed him to call for her at the house, despite noticing Nursey Goldsmith's twitching lace curtains next door. Joan was finding that more and more men were interested in her and she was enjoying it – let the neighbours talk. She had grown used to feeling like a girl amongst the older women and like a mum to her sisters. Now she felt like a woman. And it felt good. So did swapping her apron for her best dress and make-up, and getting out of the kitchen to go on a dance or a date.

However, her newfound confidence also brought with it a certain insensitivity at times. Al, like Bob before him, was rejected rather brusquely before he had even managed a kiss with Joan. The suddenness of the termination surprised not only Al but Joan, too.

He had arranged to call for her one evening to go to the cinema and she had got ready as usual. As the day wore on, she found herself becoming less inclined to go, though. She was sitting in the armchair, waiting for his arrival and thinking that she really didn't fancy the evening ahead, when he knocked on the door. Mary let him in and, as he entered the living room, Joan made an on-the-spot decision.

Without rising from the chair, she told him, 'I don't want to come.'

Al looked down at her, his ready smile fading fast. 'Are you not feeling well?' he asked.

'I'm fine,' Joan replied. 'I just don't want to go. I don't want to go out with you any more. I'm sorry, but that's the way I feel.'

Al was crushed and didn't know what to say. After standing in the Jarmans' living room for a few moments longer, feeling foolish, he uttered a brief, 'If that's the way you feel, then . . . ' before turning and walking out.

As soon as he had gone, Joan felt wretched about the dismissive way she had treated him and vowed never to be so brusque with anyone again. He had been considerate and kind, and his feelings had clearly been hurt. Now she shared some of his pain.

Occasionally, at midweek dances, Joan would not return before Mary went out and so Sheila, now thirteen, would take on the parenting role until Joan eventually returned. The enveloping darkness, intensified by the blackout, made Sheila feel vulnerable and scared, and the responsibility of being in charge of Kath, Pat and Anne weighed heavily on her young shoulders. She would lie awake in bed, jumping at every little sound she heard – real or imaginary – and couldn't go to sleep until she heard Joan return.

While her older sisters were becoming increasingly interested in the opposite sex, Sheila was feeling quite the opposite. She was so disgusted by the thought of intimacy with men that one weekend, whilst Pierce was oiling the hinges of a squeaky door, Sheila informed him that she was going to be a nun.

Pierce took it in his stride. 'If that's what you want to do,' he replied, with only the briefest of glances in her direction.

'It is, Daddy,' she insisted. 'I think it's my vocation.' With that, she walked off, leaving behind a smiling Pierce.

Sheila hated Hailsham more than ever following Annie's death. Although Joan was coping admirably with bringing up her younger sisters, she could never replace their mum, and Sheila keenly missed the comfort of knowing that Annie was there to listen, advise and care for her whenever she needed it. Things improved, however, when Mrs Buckley and her three-year-old son, Brian, moved in to one of the upstairs bedrooms at 18 Battle Road in April 1943, after her own house in Eastbourne was hit by a bomb.

When the billeting officer approached Pierce about her moving in, he was comforted by the idea that there would be a mother present in the house whilst he was back in London during the week. Despite the extra squeeze, the girls too liked having her there, and they all got on well. Indeed, it was to Rosie Buckley that the girls ran when Woppamoose made an unexpected call to the house, looking for Frank.

Dancing and Romancing

Apart from Mary, who had been on a cinema date with him, the other girls were still frightened of the hulking soldier. When Sheila saw him lumbering down their path she sounded the alarm.

'It's Woppamoose!' she shouted. 'Hide!'

Mary raised her eyebrows while her sisters darted around the house in all directions, like panicked mice, as she went to open the door.

She found him on the doorstep, blocking out the light. 'Is Frank in?' he asked in his deep voice.

'No,' said Mary.

Woppamoose looked at her for a few moments. 'He said he'd be here.'

'Well, he is due about now,' said Mary, 'but he's not here yet.'

Woppamoose raised his hand to show a bottle of beer he was holding. 'Mind if I come in and take the top off this beer?'

Mary didn't like to refuse him so she stepped aside for him to enter, casting a quick glance down the path to see if any neighbours or passers-by were watching. In the kitchen, she handed him a bottle opener. He prised the top off his beer and took a swig. Mary looked at him, wondering if he was going to leave now, but he showed no sign of being on his way.

'Well, I'd better be getting on with the housework,' she said, hoping he would take the hint, but Woppamoose wasn't the type of man who dealt with hints.

'Mind if I wait for Frank?' he asked.

Mary just wanted him to leave but she led him into the front room and told him he could wait in the armchair. He slumped down into the soft cushions, stretched his long legs and took another swig of beer. Mary, having heard her sisters running upstairs, went up to find them.

She found them in a state of high anxiety, having explained to an amused Rosie Buckley why they were hiding.

'Is he still here? When's he going?' they whispered.

Mary did her best to pacify them – it seemed Woppamoose was harmless enough, after all – but she then noticed that one of her sisters was missing.

'Where's Joan?' she asked, only to be met with blank faces.

Downstairs in the living room, Joan had decided that the Morrison shelter, with the tablecloth draped over it, would be an ideal hiding place. However, she regretted her decision when she heard Mary walk in the room with Woppamoose.

As she peered out from under the hem of the tablecloth, she could see his big feet stretched out in front of him. She was terrified of making a noise – of even breathing too loudly – in case he lifted the cloth and found her there. For a moment, she thought of crawling out and revealing herself, but what explanation could she give? Instead, she decided that she would just have to wait until he left.

Time passed slowly, though. Five minutes, ten, fifteen . . . and Joan, too frightened to move an inch, felt her limbs aching and her heart beating so loudly that she feared Woppamoose could hear it from his chair.

Meanwhile, upstairs, Mary and Rosie were hatching a plan. Mary would go back downstairs and, after a few minutes, Rosie would call down that tea was ready. They hoped that Woppamoose would then take this as a sign to leave – it would be only polite to do so – but once again they had underestimated the big man's imperviousness to subtlety. When the call came he remained firmly seated in the armchair. Mary reiterated that it was teatime but he simply looked at her with a languid expression and asked, 'Mind if I just finish this beer?'

Mary nodded in resignation and made her way back upstairs, where she stood with her sisters, listening for any sound of his departure.

'Is he going?' Kath whispered.

'He's just finishing his beer,' Mary replied. 'You shouldn't have all run off. He's just Frank's friend.'

'He's scary,' said Pat.

'He's all right when you get to know him.'

Pat looked unconvinced. 'I don't think I want to,' she said eventually.

After several more minutes huddled together, listening at the top of the stairs, they heard a stirring as Woppamoose got up and made his way out slowly, much to their relief. As they heard the front door close behind him, the girls ran downstairs and were startled when a white-faced Joan crawled out of the shelter.

'I thought he'd never leave,' she muttered and her sisters fell about laughing.

Frank was due some leave from the army and planned to visit his sister, Mary, her husband Mel and their adopted two-year-old daughter, Dolores, in the village of Oaka-moor in Staffordshire. He asked Mary to go with him and, as usual, Mary said she would have to ask her father. She approached Pierce the following weekend.

Pierce had met Frank a few times by now and liked his easygoing way and the respect he showed to Mary. That didn't mean he wanted his eldest daughter 'running off with him', though.

'I'm not running off,' Mary protested. 'You've met Frank and you like him.'

'I barely know him,' said Pierce.

'You said you liked him.'

This was true but Pierce dug his heels in. 'You're not going,' he said. 'And that's that.'

But Mary, now eighteen, was no longer quite so ready to accept her father's conclusions.

'It would be a nice break for me,' she persisted.

'I don't know why you'd even want to go to Oaka-whatever,' said Pierce. 'What about your work?'

'I'm due some time off.'

'And your sisters? They need you.'

'They've got Joan. It'll only be for a few days.'

Pierce contemplated the matter. 'Anyhow,' he said eventually. 'How do we know he even has a sister?'

'Oh, Dad!' Mary exclaimed. 'He's not going to make that up!'

'Isn't he? He might say anything just to get you away with him for a few days.'

Mary knew she wasn't getting anywhere, so instead, changed tactics and tried to make him feel guilty.

'OK, I'll tell him you said no,' she replied, and walked off.

She didn't get far before Pierce called her back. 'Get him to ask his sister to write to me,' he said in a more conciliatory tone.

'Why?' asked a puzzled Mary.

'So that I know she exists!' said Pierce.

Frank thought it odd that Pierce wanted his sister to

write but he got her to do so anyway. In the letter, she said that she would make sure that Mary would be well looked after, if he allowed her to visit. Pierce was comforted but not enough to give his immediate permission.

Frank would visit his sister with or without Mary but, as the day drew near, Pierce continued to prevaricate. Eventually, he decided that he would accompany Mary and Frank on the first part of the journey, to London, at the weekend and they could stay overnight at Pierce's sisters' house, where he was currently living. There, he would talk to Frank about things and make his decision after that. Mary would either travel onwards with Frank to Oakamoor the following morning or return alone to Hailsham. It was hardly ideal but Mary was fairly confident that Frank would be able to turn on the charm enough for Pierce to give his permission.

After travelling up to London by train in May 1943, Mary and Frank spent the evening with her father and her aunts and, although it all seemed to go well, Pierce didn't bring up the subject of the trip at all. Then, when they retired for the night, Mary was amused to find that, due to a shortage of beds, Frank would be sharing with her father! Frank was less amused but appreciated that it provided an unusual opportunity for them to bond with one another.

That night, as the two men lay side by side in bed, with their backs to each other – and as close to the edges of the bed as they could possibly get – they did have a conversation about Mary. With both of them feeling rather awkward in the circumstances, it didn't last long.

The next morning, Mary was delighted when Pierce said that she could go. She hugged her father warmly, thanking him over and over. Later, she asked Frank what they had said to each other that night in bed.

'Not much,' said Frank. 'I started talking to him about my sister and the next moment I heard him snoring!'

Mary and Frank travelled up from London to Stoke-on-Trent and then on to Oakamoor and family. It felt exciting to Mary to have this newfound independence and experience of spending quality time with her first proper boyfriend, away from the watchful eye of Pierce and the people of Hailsham. She felt properly grown up.

Frank's sister and her husband were welcoming hosts and the week's stay with them was a refreshing break. They spent much of their time going for walks in the hazy spring sunshine, just the two of them, getting to know each other better day by day and becoming closer.

Mary was confused, however, when, on one of their long walks, Frank made a strange request.

'Mary, would you mind if I gave you a ring to wear?' he asked. Mary's mind started to race and she felt her heart pumping. She stopped to look at him, wondering just what was coming next.

'This one,' he said, pulling a signet ring from his little finger. Mary was puzzled. 'If you could wear it on your wedding finger . . . ' he went on.

'My *wedding* finger? What are you saying, Frank?'

Frank looked uncharacteristically sheepish. 'There's this girl, you see . . . ' he began.

'What girl?' Mary snapped.

'A girl that I sometimes see when I visit my sister.'

Mary was not liking this.

'It's nothing serious. Just a friend, really. We just meet up and . . . '

'And what?'

'Just, you know, go to the cinema. Just friends, that's all,' Frank explained.

'So why do you want me to wear your ring?' Mary's voice was frosty.

'My sister told this girl that I was visiting again but that I was bringing you.'

'So?' Mary was determined not to make this easy for Frank.

'Well, she, er . . . added that we were engaged.'

'Whatever for?' asked Mary, genuinely perplexed.

Frank explained that now he was seeing *her*, he no longer wanted to hang out with the other girl, and that his sister had taken it upon herself to tell the girl that Frank now had a fiancée.

Mary was finding it difficult to take it all in. 'But she's just a friend?' she asked.

'Yeah but . . . probably a little keen,' he said with an awkward smile.

Despite finding it all rather odd, Mary agreed to wear the ring in case they bumped into her. They never did. The whole episode made Mary realize that perhaps Frank wasn't entirely what he appeared to be – but the idea that there might be another girl interested in him only made her all the more keen.

Their stay in Oakamoor was all too brief for Mary's liking. She hadn't had any kind of holiday for years, and just as she was starting to really unwind, it was time to return home.

She soon forgot she was still wearing Frank's ring but when she took it off to give it back to him ahead of returning to London, he asked if she would keep it on. When she asked why, Frank replied that he liked the feeling of them being engaged, adding, 'I'll get you a proper engagement ring when I can.'

It took a moment for this rather casual comment to sink in. When it did, Mary realized that this was Frank's version of a marriage proposal. It was hardly Prince Charming and Cinderella, or indeed anything like she had seen in the romantic Hollywood films but, nevertheless, she couldn't help but smile.

A tingle of excitement ran through her body. When she had agreed to wear Frank's old signet ring, she'd had no idea that it would ruin any dreams she might have harboured about one day having a romantic, down-on-one-knee style, traditional marriage proposal. But this was good enough for her. More than good enough. She was delighted.

'I'll have to ask my dad,' she said.

It was Frank's turn to smile. 'He'll be fine. We've shared a bed.'

Mary suspected that Pierce would not be caught up in the romance of it all, though, and she was nervous telling him about it when they had returned home. Her fears were well founded.

'Certainly not,' he said. 'You're only eighteen. Wait until you're twenty-one.'

'It just means we're engaged, that's all,' said Mary. 'I'm not about to leave home.'

Pierce felt himself shudder at the thought. 'He could be off with the army at any moment. He lives in Canada, Mary. Would you want to live there?'

'No, of course not,' said Mary. 'It's just a sign of commitment.'

Dancing and Romancing

'A commitment unlikely to last,' said Pierce. 'He's a soldier and a Canadian.'

The lively conversation continued in this vein for a while longer before Mary gave up. She kept the ring on, though, and bided her time with Pierce, comforted by the fact that the band symbolized that she and Frank were engaged whether her father liked it or not.

Nine-year-old Pat was to have a fortuitous encounter with a solider – an American one – when she was walking along the High Street with two of her friends. Ahead of them were two American soldiers with their English girlfriends. Such sights were frowned upon occasionally by men not on the war front. A common complaint amongst British men at the time about the 'Yanks' was that they were 'overpaid, oversexed and over 'ere'. Pat had good reason on this occasion to be pleased about them being overpaid because as one of the soldiers reached into his pocket to take out his handkerchief, several coins – pennies, as well as sixpences – fell out and rolled away on the pavement.

To the girls' astonishment, the soldier just looked down at what had happened, shrugged and carried on walking.

'Come on!' said Pat, wide-eyed with excitement. 'He doesn't want it!' She led the way in bending down and scooping up the money quickly. The friends shared out their windfall, sixpence each. Sweets were rationed but children, as well as adults, had learnt to find alternatives. Cough drops, Fisherman's Friends and Zubes would not have been their usual choice of delight but they were classified as medicinal and therefore not rationed, and were easily available at the chemist. So off they set to satisfy their sugar craving.

*

The aunts continued to visit the girls regularly and would rebuke them sharply if they thought that their housekeeping didn't meet their own standards. The girls would clean and tidy the house furiously before their aunts arrived, polishing the woodwork, sweeping the floors and dusting from top to bottom. Their aunts would walk from room to room, checking for dust and dirt like sergeant majors inspecting the barracks of the rank and file. It was rarely good enough, despite the girls' best efforts.

Notwithstanding the often cold behaviour towards the girls by their aunts, Sheila, now thirteen, was thrilled when Pierce finally agreed to let her stay with his sisters in London one weekend in the summer of 1943. He had been reticent because of the risk of bombing but Sheila had continued to ask him over the years and, realizing now just how homesick she was, he relented finally. What's more, Mary had recently made a blue dress for her, which Sheila loved and felt very grown up in when she tried it on, so she decided to pack it for her stay in London, imagining how her aunts would approve of it and how she might do them proud.

She was going to travel alone on the train to London and Mary had given her 2 shillings and sixpence for her fare and any additional expenses. Pierce, who was down for the weekend as usual, accompanied her to the station early on Saturday morning, and Sheila felt a rush of exhilaration when she boarded the train, smiling and waving goodbye to her father from the carriage window.

Her excitement about her London adventure increased as the journey progressed, and she thought about experiencing the familiar sights and smells again. Once the train had shuddered to a laborious halt at London

Bridge station, amidst billowing steam, she stepped sprightly onto the platform, bag in hand.

None of the aunts had planned to meet her at the station, but Sheila wasn't worried. She made her way cheerfully and confidently down the steps from the station but instead of turning right along Tooley Street, she turned left by mistake and found herself on Borough High Street. It was a while before she realized that she was going the wrong way and, as her steps faltered, she began to fret. Disorientated, she eventually asked a woman if she could tell her the way to Stanworth Street and the woman helpfully gave her directions. Back on track, she smiled to herself once more as she began to recognize familiar buildings.

Bermondsey may have been grey and dirty but it was home to Sheila and her mind turned to four years earlier – it seemed like a lifetime ago – when she had last seen Tooley Street. Then, she had been walking the other way, towards London Bridge with her fellow school pupils, sisters and mother, leaving for a new life in the countryside. Her mother. Who would have thought back then that the war would still be on and that she would be making the return journey with her mother gone? It all seemed so incredible and unreal and, overcome by the strange turn life had taken, she became tearful. Quickly dabbing at her eyes with her handkerchief she made a point of looking up and around her, to see how things had changed.

Dockhead was largely how she remembered it – the houses, pubs, shops – but there were also big differences. She passed several bomb-damaged buildings, some no more than piles of rubble, and eventually arrived at the family home in Abbey Street. Or what was left of it. It too had been hit badly – something Sheila knew, of course, but was still almost surprised to see before her. She felt a sudden anger that an anonymous German pilot could have done this to the house where she and her family had shared so many experiences; the house which had been the very fabric of their lives. It seemed obscene to target this home of love and memories.

She felt sorry for her family and sorry for the building itself, for the very brickwork that had once been so special to them. Sheila stood staring at the destruction for a few minutes, touched by the sight of chunks of fallen wall still bearing scraps of familiar wallpaper, before moving away slowly. She felt as though another chapter in their lives had truly ended. There really was no going back to the way things used to be. They were different people now.

Aunt Rose opened the door to Sheila at the house in Stanworth Street.

'Come in. We expected you earlier. Where have you been?' she asked. Before Sheila had a chance to reply, her aunt added, 'We're going into Peckham this afternoon, to look around some shops. Fancy that?'

Sheila was delighted, albeit a little less so when Rose added, 'You *have* got some money, haven't you?'

Her Aunt Nell then appeared, unsmiling. Noticing Sheila's bag, she commented, 'Do you want to unpack your things in the bedroom?'

Sheila smiled for the first time since arriving, feeling a warm pleasure as she remembered the new dress that Mary had made for her and which she had so carefully folded and packed. She couldn't wait to show it off and now was the opportunity to do so.

'Oh yes,' she replied. 'I really do need to hang up my new dress.'

Dancing and Romancing

In the bedroom, she placed her bag on a chair, opened it up and unfolded her pretty blue dress with pride. She held it up for her aunts to see. However, Sheila's hopes that her aunts would think the dress as lovely as she did, and make nice comments about it, were dashed. Even when she put it on later and stood there, expecting that they must notice it, there was no reaction from them. Sheila thought to herself how much fuss her mother would have made over her, with her ringlets and new outfit, and felt yet another pang of longing for Annie.

Nonetheless, on their bus journey into Peckham, Sheila felt very pretty and was sure that fellow passengers were giving her admiring looks. She wasn't going to let her aunts bring her down – she was in London, she was wearing her new blue dress and, just for the moment, life felt really exciting.

Two of the aunts' favourite shopping destinations were the elegant department stores: Jones and Higgins – the most prestigious shop in Peckham – and Holdron's. The two establishments on Rye Lane were part of South London's Golden Mile of shopping paradise and the women could easily spend over an hour inside each one, looking at all the different items on sale – a vast array of glassware, furniture, ornaments, linen. It was all rather too highly priced for them to consider actually buying anything but they enjoyed looking nevertheless.

As they hovered next to a highly polished dining-room table and chairs, agreeing how beautiful it all looked, a shop assistant approached and asked if they would like any help. Sheila smiled to herself as her aunts began their well-rehearsed charade.

'We're just looking at the moment,' said Rose.

The assistant left them alone for a while and then, when she returned, Mary said, 'We're not sure. We can't make up our mind.'

Then Nell added, with an air of finality, 'We'd best go home and ask Charlie first. See what he thinks.' With that, they would walk away.

There was, of course, no Charlie, but they didn't want anyone to think that they couldn't afford what was on offer.

Sheila bought some sweets in the High Street with her own money but her aunts did treat her to a cake at Lyons tea shop, which was a favourite stop of theirs. There they would sit and feel very grand, being served by waitresses in black dresses with twin columns of pearl buttons running down the front to the waist, white collars and cuffs, aprons and black-and-white frilly hats. The waitresses were known colloquially as Nippies, most likely for the speed at which they would nip around, taking and serving orders. Sheila looked at their waitress, thinking how elegant she looked and how nice it must be to dress up like that every day for work.

That evening Sheila was told to squeeze in with her aunts in their bed, which she hated doing. However, it was worth enduring, on balance, for a pleasurable weekend that included the aunts' traditional home-made cake, which was either made with coconut or, on this occasion, caraway seed. Sheila loved the light taste and the delicate aroma and, as filling as it was, it was always followed by fruit salad and cream – and then a slice of bread and butter because, according to the aunts' strange logic, the cake and fruit and cream were 'too rich to have on their own'. Unfortunately, it was then time for the equally traditional

Sunday afternoon nap, for which she had to squeeze into bed with her aunts once more!

Sheila's weekend away flew by and on the train home alone, she felt sad at the thought of leaving Bermondsey and returning to Hailsham.

Pierce got on well with Rosie Buckley. The pair would chat together in the kitchen when she was either on her way out, or returning to the house. It was nice to have another adult around whom he could talk to about the sort of things that were occupying everyone's minds – such as the progress of the war and food rationing – but also to seek advice occasionally about the needs and concerns of his daughters. They needed a 'motherly' presence and Rosie was a godsend.

It had been two years since Annie had died. Rosie, whose husband was away fighting with the army, was an attractive lady and although Pierce had not failed to notice that, his thoughts returned constantly to his wife of seventeen years and their shared experiences.

Pierce was the target of a romantic overture from another woman. The kindly Miss Hunt, who had taken it upon herself to look in on the Jarman girls now that Annie was no longer around, revealed a secondary motive for her frequent visits. She had taken a shine to Pierce and would often drop by the house at weekends when he was there. At first Pierce couldn't quite understand why she was calling – he'd certainly done nothing to encourage her – but it began to dawn on him slowly why she kept popping round. She would look at him in a certain way, with a shy little smile that made him feel uncomfortable, because, unfortunately, the romantic feelings he aroused in her were not reciprocated.

Mary and Joan had also noticed how Miss Hunt became quite girly in Pierce's presence and were amused both by that and by their father's unease. They had become used to Miss Hunt asking them regularly during the week, 'Is your father coming down this weekend?' Then, when he arrived on a Friday evening and they told him she had been asking about him, he would become rather agitated.

Eventually, he asked Mary and Joan rather sheepishly if they would tell Miss Hunt that he wouldn't be visiting at the weekend – even when he was – but she invariably saw him out and about anyway. To his alarm, she even began waiting for him at the bus station.

One chilly Saturday in the late days of summer 1943, he saw her walking towards the house, and decided to take drastic action.

'I'll be in the garden, girls!' he said hurriedly. 'Miss Hunt's arriving. Tell her I'm not here.' As he was heading out, he called back, 'And tell me when she's gone!'

Joan opened the door to Miss Hunt, trying hard not to laugh.

'Hello, Joan, just thought I'd pop round to see how you are,' she said, walking in. 'Is Daddy down?'

'No, he's not here this weekend, Miss Hunt,' Joan lied. 'He's having to work.'

'Oh,' said Miss Hunt, obviously disappointed. Joan felt that she had to offer her a cup of tea, as usual, and Miss Hunt accepted.

Meanwhile, out in the garden, Pierce was crouched down, hiding behind a bush. It was a chilly day and in his rush to escape, he had had no time to put on a cardigan or coat over his shirt, and now he was regretting it. In fact, he was regretting his rash move altogether because not only did he feel cold, he also felt foolish, and had no idea how long Miss Hunt was going to stay.

Inside, Miss Hunt was enjoying her cup of tea and nattering away with Joan, even if she was disappointed that Pierce wasn't there. Aware of her father outside, Joan tried not to engage her in conversation too much but Miss Hunt always had plenty to say about what was going on in the area and who was doing what. Annie had always had time for her because she thought it must be a little dull for her at home with just her father for company, and so Joan tried to behave as her mother would have done. She listened politely, asked some questions and made some remarks here and there. However, after half an hour, Joan had become increasingly worried about her father. When she heard Mary coming in through the side door, she got up.

'Will you excuse me for a moment, Miss Hunt?' she said and walked out to the kitchen.

'Mary,' she whispered. 'Will you take Daddy his coat?'

'Where is he?' asked a puzzled Mary.

'Shhh . . . He's hiding in the garden.'

'Hiding in the . . . '

'From Miss Hunt.' Joan explained hurriedly in whispered tones what had happened, as Mary began to giggle. It was too absurd for words.

'Be quiet, Mary,' Joan admonished. 'She'll hear you.'

'OK, OK,' said Mary, but she had to hold a hand over her mouth in an attempt to stifle her laughter as Joan walked back into the living room.

'Is that Mary?' asked Miss Hunt.

'Yes, she's just . . . erm, in and out.'

'I *thought* I heard her laughing.' She smiled. 'She's always laughing at something.'

In the garden, Mary saw the white shirt on the curve of her father's back as he crouched under a bush, and started laughing again.

'What *are* you doing?' she asked her father.

Pierce jumped. 'Mary!' he said, looking up. 'You startled me.'

'I brought you your coat,' she said, handing it to him.

'Thank God!' he said as he put it on quickly, trying to control his shivers. 'When is she leaving?' he whispered.

'I don't know,' Mary replied. 'She always stays quite a while. You know what she's like.'

Miss Hunt remained in the living room for over an hour before finally taking her leave. As soon as she did so, Pierce was given the all-clear. He walked back into the house with aching limbs and a cross expression on his face.

'I thought she'd never leave,' he said. 'It's freezing out there.'

The girls couldn't contain their laughter any longer.

'Serves you right for running away!' Mary teased. It felt strange for her to be behaving like the adult for once and her father like a child.

CHAPTER 8

War Bride

Frank and Mary on their wedding day at the convent in Dockhead, Bermondsey.

THE JARMANS' NEIGHBOURS in Hailsham assumed that, in the absence of the girls' mother, their aunts were their chief carers, and that's certainly what their regular visits from London suggested to the outside world. In reality, although the aunts would occasionally do some cooking and shopping, the girls did most of it themselves, even when their aunts were there. They were bringing themselves up, and they went to a lot of trouble to assure Pierce that they were doing a good job.

Despite Sheila's attachment to Bermondsey, without realizing it the Jarman girls had gradually become country girls, and even tomboy Kath had got to know the names of various plants, trees and flowers. She had learnt most of them from Miss Mobbs, who would take the class on a weekly nature trail. The route took them across the rec and over a stile into a field where they could follow various pathways. As they walked along, they would stop every now and then for Miss Mobbs to identify the various plant life.

'Those feather-shaped leaves, there,' she would say, pointing. 'That's wild parsley.' A little while later she might draw their attention to 'yellow bell-shaped flowers', explaining that they were cowslip.

Kath looked forward to the nature trails not only because they were far preferable to class work but also because she was genuinely interested in learning all the different names. On one particular outing, the class had crossed the rec and climbed over the stile when, a little way down one of the paths, they saw a horse in a clearing. The children stopped in their tracks as it looked at them, only a few yards away.

'Come along, children,' called Miss Mobbs from behind. 'It's just a horse. It's not going to hurt you.'

Barely were the words out of her mouth when the horse bolted suddenly and made a few strides towards them. As the children screamed and turned back in their tracks, they were surprised to see their teacher ahead of them, in a shameless show of 'every man for himself', making a run for the stile and clambering swiftly to safety, leaving her charges to follow in her wake.

Once they were all back in the rec, a wide-eyed and slightly breathless Miss Mobbs tried to regain her equilibrium and said, with as much dignity as she could muster, 'I think we should go elsewhere for our nature trail today, children.' With that, they set off afresh, the children sniggering as they followed behind their not-so-esteemed leader.

Shortly after this incident Kath got into trouble at school and for once she was innocent. Her classmate and fellow Dockhead evacuee, Pamela Phillips, had removed her hairband and asked Kath if she would hold it for a moment while she rearranged her hair. As Kath took the band, Miss Mobbs caught sight of her.

'Stand up, Kath Jarman!' she shouted. Kath did so and the teacher approached and smacked her sharply on the leg.

'Now go and stand outside until I tell you to come back in!' she said.

A startled and tearful Kath did as she was told, but wondered what she had done to incur such wrath. After being outside for a while on her own, Kath became frightened when she thought she heard the distant sound of an aeroplane engine. Miss Mobbs still hadn't called her to come back in and Kath, on the spur of the moment, decided that she would go home.

Running off, she was met at home by Uncle Albert, Pierce's younger brother, who was visiting. A kindly man, with a mild and good-natured disposition – and an endless supply of puns – he was upset to see Kath so distraught.

'I'm not going back. I hate her,' said Kath, as the tears burst forth. 'She made me stand outside with the planes going over.'

'Come and sit down and tell me all about it,' he said, quietly wondering what planes she was referring to, as he hadn't heard anything.

Kath explained to him in detail what had happened. She fully expected him to send her straight back to school, as her father would have done, so was relieved and grateful when Albert told her that she could stay at home for the rest of the day.

The following morning, Kath's indignation had abated, and although she still felt aggrieved by the incident at school, she was worried about what Miss Mobbs would say to her about her disappearance. To her surprise, her teacher didn't say a word about it and Kath wondered whether once she had told her to stand outside she had simply forgotten all about her.

When Kath moved on from being taught by Miss Mobbs and started secondary school at the age of eleven in

September 1943, she found it as challenging as her older sisters had done. They were all painfully aware by now that the level of education they had received at their schools in Bermondsey was far below the expected standard in Hailsham, and it was difficult for them to catch up.

English was her favourite subject and she liked the teacher, Mrs Russell. However, she was less keen on the history teacher, Miss Foster, whom Kath considered a rather austere, straight-backed woman, and whose severe-looking brogues completed a rather unsympathetic look. Kath felt that she frequently criticized the London children for their lack of knowledge and, despite the passage of time, she still considered them outsiders.

'She doesn't like evacuees,' she told Pierce.

'I'm sure she does,' he replied. 'Joan always got on very well with her. She thought her very nice.'

Despite her father's reassurance, the following day at school, Kath was dismayed when Miss Foster went round the class, providing the origin of each pupil's surname. Kath was looking forward to her turn but felt humiliated when Miss Foster dismissed her with, 'Jarman. Oh, just a common town name.'

Kath was invariably bottom of the class in history tests and was dejected each time she checked the results list pinned to the notice board. She knew that she would arrive at her name soonest if she looked at the end of the list first. Usually her name was right at the bottom but just occasionally, and to her great delight, it came one or two places above. One day, however, she couldn't see her name in the usual spot and so slowly worked her way upwards and upwards – but still couldn't find it. Beginning to think that it must have been left off by mistake, she carried on working her way up towards the top where, to her astonishment, she saw that she was in second place, just behind Gordon Alchorn, who was always in first place and was never beaten.

Kath felt her heart beating quickly with excitement. She sat down at her desk, wide-eyed with wonder, bursting with pride and eagerly anticipating the words of praise Miss Foster would finally give her for what was a remarkable achievement. To her great disappointment, Miss Foster didn't say a word.

'What's the matter?' Joan asked her when she returned home that afternoon with a face like thunder.

'I hate that Miss Foster!' Kath stormed.

'She's nice, Kath,' said Joan.

'That's what you think,' Kath replied as she stomped upstairs and threw herself onto her bed. Lying there, her thoughts turned to comforting memories of her primary school, St Joseph's, in Bermondsey.

There, little camp beds were set up in the hallway in the afternoon for the children to have a sleep, and their daily bottle of milk was warmed up on a black range in the corner of the classroom. Kath smiled to herself as she also recalled the spoonful of malt extract, given to them each day by school helper Mrs Watt, who was also known amongst the children as 'the malt lady'. It was thought to be of nutritional benefit and they would line up every morning by the first-aid office near the dinner hall, where Mrs Watt would dip a spoon in the sweet, syrupy substance, roll it around until it had stopped dripping and then pop it into the mouth of each child in turn. It wasn't hygienic and not everyone liked it but Kath did, and even now she could not only taste the thick sweetness but also smell the strong malty aroma. It was an enormously comforting memory but the reality of daily life at secondary school was still all too real.

Outside of school, Kath's burgeoning career as a 'thief' reached a new level when one evening she saw Mary's Land Army satchel hanging over the back of the kitchen chair. Kath knew that money was tight in the house – they all did – and she didn't like to keep asking Joan or Mary for spare coins. Now she was faced with temptation.

She was on her own. Furtively looking about her to check that no one else was around, she peeked inside the bag and, as expected, saw Mary's purse inside. Kath felt that familiar surge of blood to her head, just as she had in Bainbridge's shop. Just a shilling. That's all. Mary wouldn't miss it. It would be easy. And so it was. Quickly dipping into the purse, light-fingered Kath took the silver coin and placed the satchel back on the chair before making a swift getaway.

Having taken the money, Kath now had no idea what to do with it. Her intention was not to spend it on herself. That would be wrong and selfish. But what would she do? The truth is Kath hadn't thought that far ahead. In the heat of the moment, her mind had been focused simply on taking the money. She had no idea what for.

For the rest of that evening she felt her tummy knot with twin threads of guilt and nerves. What if Mary *did* notice? By the following morning, she was resolved about what to do and marched down to the greengrocer's, determined to buy food for the family with the shilling.

'It's like Robin Hood,' she comforted herself. 'Stealing

from the rich to give to the poor.' Although she secretly knew that the analogy was as quivery as the outlaw's bowstring, she felt that her actions would benefit everyone in the end.

At the shop, she shrugged off almost all of her remaining guilt by deciding that she would buy something special. A treat. Amongst the dusty greenery and earthy potatoes, a display of gleaming yellow corncobs stood out. That's it, she thought. They had never had corn on the cob. Now was the time. Wouldn't everyone be pleased? Kath bought a bagful with the shilling and carried it home, smiling. She had already thought of what to say when confronted with Joan's inevitable question . . .

'Where did you get them from?' asked Joan, peering into the bag.

'Rita gave them to me. Said her dad had loads,' said a well-rehearsed Kath.

Joan looked at her sister. 'That's very generous,' she said. 'I must thank her mum when I see her.'

Kath froze. She hadn't foreseen that. Recovering quickly, she said, 'There's no need. I thanked Rita already.'

'Still,' said Joan. 'I need to thank her mum. It's only polite.'

'I can thank her,' said an increasingly anxious Kath.

Joan furrowed her brow. 'You can thank her. You should. But I will thank her too,' she said, adding, somewhat to her surprise, 'because that's what mothers do.'

Realizing that she was getting nowhere and that further debate would draw suspicion, Kath sloped off, cursing herself for not anticipating this turn of events.

Joan cooked the corn that evening and Kath's unease about being exposed as a thief and a liar simmered temporarily, rather than boiled, as she glowed in the warmth of the golden cobs being served to her sisters, all sitting in eager anticipation of this treat, provided by her. However, her siblings' appreciative comments as they crunched into the corn, although welcome, didn't fill her with as much delight as might have been expected because, to her dismay, Kath found that she didn't like the taste of the corn at all!

Kath's lie about Rita was a good one because her friend frequently gave her food for cookery lessons at school. Kath enjoyed these classes but always fretted because the children were expected to take in their own ingredients and Kath knew that there was barely enough money at home to buy sufficient food for their daily needs. Feeling embarrassed about the situation, Kath began to tell her teacher a little lie – that she had forgotten to bring the food in.

Kath knocked customarily for Rita on her way to school and, becoming aware that Kath frequently had no food for cookery lessons, Rita would help her out whenever she could, particularly with fruit because her father had an orchard.

'Have you got your apples?' Rita asked, when Kath knocked for her the day that they were due to make an apple pie in class. An uncomfortable-looking Kath mumbled that she had forgotten to bring them and so Rita went back inside to get some for her.

A few days later, after the corn had been devoured by everyone else but Kath, Joan was on her way to the shops when she saw Rita's mother on the other side of the road.

'Oh, Mrs Wood!' she called, and walked across to her. 'Thank you so much for giving our Kath the vegetables.'

Mrs Wood looked at Joan blankly before realizing

what she was alluding to – or rather, what she *thought* she was alluding to. 'That's all right, dear,' she said with a smile. 'We've plenty of apples.'

They parted ways, with Joan wondering what on earth apples had to do with it and Mrs Wood thinking that perhaps Joan thought apples were vegetables. Much to her relief, Kath's little misdemeanour remained undetected.

Mary continued to find working life on the farm something of an ordeal but all that changed when, without any warning, Mr Burton told her and Barbara that he was selling out to the Co-op, explaining, 'I'm getting too old for this malarkey.'

'What will happen to us?' Mary asked, concerned for her job.

'Well, that's up to them,' he replied.

In the event, the new Co-op manager asked Mary to stay on – to accompany their milkman on his horse and cart, and to show him the route and houses of the customers he needed to deliver to. Mary was delighted to be back on the road and safely away from the cows. Things got even better for her when a little while later she was offered another Land Army job as a permanent milk-lorry driver at Highlands Farm in Hailsham, owned by Mr Willoughby. She was relieved to find Mr Willoughby, unlike Mr Burton, a pleasure to work for. He was always very cordial and greeted her readily with a 'Good morning!' and a smile. 'He's a real gentleman,' she told Pierce, who nodded his approval.

But life here, too, was to have its challenges for Mary.

It was fine being on the road, doing the milk deliveries, but time spent on the farm itself was never pleasant as far as she was concerned. Not only did farm animals scare her but she was also terrified by the tiny field mice that would scurry around her feet when she was out in the fields digging up swedes and scraping them clean for cattle feeding. Even worse were the rats that ran around when Mary was helping to pitchfork the crops into haystacks prior to loading them into the threshing machine. She would think back longingly to her time at Koupy Gowns, a period of relative ease that now felt like a lifetime ago.

During busy times, the Canadian soldiers would help out on the farm as part of the war effort and proved most useful in whacking the rats with sticks. In an attempt to put distance between herself and the rodents, Mary volunteered to stand on top of the haystack, dragging the crops up with a pitchfork and levelling them out on top as those below added more and more to the pile.

However, she was so intent on her work one afternoon that she didn't realize just how high the stack had become. When it was time to come down, although one of the soldiers placed a ladder up the side of the stack for her, she was unable to reach the top rung with her foot. As she struggled in an ungainly fashion, with her leg dangling over the edge of the stack, feeling blindly for the ladder, the soldiers laughed at her predicament until one of them climbed up and gallantly helped her down.

As well as being well looked after by the soldiers, Mary also felt as though she had a father at work as well as at home, for Mr Willoughby had taken it upon himself to guard her morals. As far as Mary was concerned, that was definitely one father too many. She would often walk part of the way to work with a girl who lived a few doors away from her. They had met at the Silverlight Laundry, where the girl still worked, but she had something of a reputation and Mr Willoughby didn't like the idea of Mary mixing with her. When he asked to see Mary in his office, she wondered what he could possibly want, especially when she saw his serious expression.

'Just wanted a quick word . . . in private,' he said.

Mary waited but the 'quick word' took a while in coming.

'There's a girl,' he began, in a lower tone, 'who I hear you walk part of the way to work with in the mornings.'

'Oh yes?' said Mary.

'She . . . she . . . isn't your friend, is she?' he said, squirming uncomfortably in his seat.

'Well, we're not best friends but we know each other and I like her,' Mary replied.

'But you don't . . . socialize with her?'

'No.'

Mr Willoughby took a deep breath. 'I'd sooner you not be seen with her because she's not a very nice girl.'

Mary knew what he was referring to. She too had heard that her old work mate worked as a prostitute. Annie had also known. In fact, most local people did. Annie had not been judgmental, though, and had liked her because she thought she was a kind girl. If she had been good enough for Annie, then that was good enough for Mary. As she didn't feel that she could argue with Mr Willoughby, her employer, she just nodded and left his office. Nevertheless, she continued to see the girl. It wasn't a good idea to tell a Jarman what to do. Mary was most definitely her mother's daughter.

In early 1944, one of the Canadian soldiers gave Mary a hen, which he said they had been keeping in their camp.

Mary didn't know how they had come to have it, or quite why they wanted to get rid of it, but she thought it would be useful for supplying eggs for the family and so she took it home in a cardboard box. Pierce was pleased when he saw it and made a cage in the garden.

'We should have a nice supply of fresh eggs soon,' he said. However, as the weeks went on and there was no sign of any eggs, Pierce began to get frustrated. Then he thought of another use for the hen.

'When I come down next weekend, I'll kill that chicken and we can have it for Sunday dinner,' he declared.

The comment was met with a stunned silence, followed by wails of protest from his daughters.

'You can't do that!'

'I'm not eating her!'

'That's cruel!'

'It's a *chicken*!' Pierce exclaimed. 'It's a meal. Don't be silly, girls. It'll be a nice treat for us next Sunday.'

For the rest of that week the girls were worried sick at the thought of their father killing the hen. Mary knew all too well how Daddy liked his meat and that he wasn't always so keen to have eggs – neither she nor her sisters would ever forget the time back home in Abbey Street when he didn't get the steak he was expecting for dinner.

On Fridays, one of Mary's jobs had been to go to the local fish and chip shop to buy the weekly family treat. Fish was tuppence a piece and chips were a penny a portion. The shop counter was so high that she couldn't be seen over it and so had to jump up and down, shouting out the order that Annie had written on a note for her. What's more, she also had to suffer the indignity of being told by the woman who served there not to make such a noise.

Pierce wasn't keen on fish and chips, and so each week he would put sixpence on the mantelpiece for Annie to buy him some steak instead. What Pierce didn't know was that Annie, intrigued by her brother Mike's success in betting on the horses, had started to give the sixpence to him to place a bet for her. Her early successes emboldened her until, inevitably, she lost. Worried sick about not having any money for Pierce's steak and that he would find out she had gambled his sixpence away, she hoped she could give him egg and chips instead, and that he wouldn't notice. Unfortunately, Pierce looked forward to his Friday-night treat more than she realized. When she'd placed his meal on the table, he'd stared at it and asked bluntly, 'Where's my steak?'

'I thought you'd like a change,' she replied.

Pierce looked up at her. 'I don't fancy a change. I left the money for steak.'

'Well, I was a bit short this week,' she said.

'You shouldn't have been short,' he argued. 'I left sixpence for steak, not eggs!'

As the row escalated, the girls all sat in silence around the kitchen table, surprised to hear their father standing his ground. However, it was Annie who, as usual, had the final word. Fed up with his moaning she took decisive action.

Picking up his plate, she shouted, 'Well, if you don't want it, don't bloody have it!' and hurled it at her husband.

Pierce had ducked just in time and the plate hit the wall above the fireplace. The girls watched open-mouthed as the fried egg slid slowly and dramatically down the wall. Pierce stormed out and time seemed to stand still in the room. The incident scared them at the time but they later giggled about it – the image of the descending egg would stay with them for a lifetime.

Now, with Pierce having set his mind on roast chicken the following Sunday, Mary and her sisters knew that their hen's days were numbered. Drastic action was required and so they all agreed with Mary's decision to return the hen to the Canadians.

The following weekend, when Pierce went out into the garden on Sunday morning, the girls exchanged worried looks with each other. After a few minutes, he re-entered the house with a puzzled expression.

'Where's that bloody chicken?' he asked his nervous daughters.

Mary and Joan stood shoulder to shoulder.

'It's gone back to where it came from,' said Mary, putting on a bold front.

'You've given our dinner away?' Pierce asked.

As Mary nodded apprehensively, Joan tried to explain to her father. 'We couldn't eat that chicken, Dad,' she said. 'It was our pet.'

Pierce just stared at her for a moment or two before shaking his head and walking away. So much for them becoming country girls!

In March 1944, Frank told Mary he had a funny feeling that the Canadian troops would be moving on soon. He was right. Plans for a secret Allied invasion of Normandy had been in discussion for some time and military manoeuvres amongst the troops had been stepped up. It wasn't long before Frank had some firm news for Mary.

'How long will you be gone?' she asked him as they took a stroll through the rec, arm in arm.

'Who knows?' he replied. 'Weeks, months . . . longer.'

They walked in silence for a while, both deep in thought about the future. *Their* future.

'Maybe you won't return . . . ' Mary mused. Frank glanced at her and she quickly added, 'You might decide not to come back.'

Frank reassured her that he would return and that he wouldn't have given her an engagement ring if he didn't want them to have a future together. Mary looked down at his thin signet ring on her finger, running her thumb across its surface. It lacked the romance and beauty of a proper engagement ring but she supposed it was a commitment – of sorts.

'Let's sit down for a while,' she said as they came to a bench overlooking the pond.

'Do you want to get married, Frank?' she asked, staring out at the ducks on the water.

'Of course. You have my ring, don't you?'

'But when?' Mary pressed.

'As soon as the war is over.'

Mary looked at him and said, 'We have no idea when that might be. I want us to be married, Frank . . . before you leave.'

Frank thought about this for a few moments. 'I don't know if we have time, Mary,' he said.

'But do you want to?'

Frank smiled. 'Of course!' he exclaimed, leaning over to give her a kiss.

'I want to get married in Dockhead,' she said. 'Where Mummy and Daddy married.'

'But wasn't that church bombed?' he asked.

'Yes, but they're using the convent next to it for masses and weddings.'

'Fine,' said Frank. 'But we'd best get a move on.'

Mary's mind immediately filled with happy thoughts and wedding plans but she knew that the conversation with her father about it was likely to be tricky.

'You'd be a fool to marry him right now,' said Pierce. 'If he's going off fighting abroad, who knows what might happen.' He paused. 'You might find yourself a widow. At eighteen!'

Mary felt tears welling in her eyes at the thought but it made her even more determined to marry the man she had fallen in love with. 'I'd regret it then, if we hadn't married,' she replied.

Pierce shook his head. 'Just wait, Mary. There's no rush.'

'But there is, Daddy. We want to marry before he leaves.'

Eventually, fed up with arguing with his eldest daughter and feeling like he couldn't make her see sense, Pierce said that they would talk about it later. His delay tactics made no difference to Mary's position, though. He realized he wasn't ever going to change her mind and so, after one more attempt to talk her round, he gave his blessing, despite his reservations.

As soon as they could, Mary and Frank travelled up to London where they met the parish priest to make arrangements to marry.

'It takes time to arrange these things,' Father Spillane told them, as they sat in the presbytery. He gave a little shake of his head. 'Months, not weeks.' Mary felt her face drop as he leafed through an appointments book. 'However,' he added, glancing up at them. 'I do have a cancellation.'

Mary was startled by his reply. 'When?' she asked eagerly.

'Next Saturday,' he said.

Mary looked at Frank.

'Other than that, it couldn't happen until late summer,' Father Spillane explained.

Frank gave Mary a little nod. 'We'll take it,' she said.

They bought a marriage licence for 7 shillings and sixpence and Mary spent her journey back to Hailsham wondering nervously what her father was going to say about the wedding taking place so soon, and how she was going to get herself prepared in time. What on earth was she going to wear?

Mary and Frank's wedding was set for 1 April 1944, a date that made Mary giggle – April Fool's Day.

Pierce, as Mary had expected, was both alarmed and cross when she broke the news to him.

'That's ridiculous, Mary,' he said. 'There's so much to do.'

'But it's the only chance we have,' she replied. 'Please, Dad. It's something we want to do. I want to marry him before he goes away.'

Pierce held his hand to his head in frustration. He didn't want to have this conversation with his daughter again, though. 'OK,' he said eventually. 'Seeing as you've set the date and bought the licence.'

Mary smiled and gave him a hug. 'It'll be fine,' she said. 'You'll see.'

Her sisters, in contrast to Pierce, were hopping with excitement at the news, particularly Sheila, who had waited a long time for Mary to get married. At least, to a girl of her age, it had seemed a long time. When the girls' cousin Kit married before the war, Sheila was going to be her bridesmaid. She was looking forward to it eagerly, only to come down with measles days before the wedding and Joan had to step into her shoes.

Mary had comforted an upset and tearful Sheila. 'Never mind. When I get married you can be *my* bridesmaid,' she promised her. Sheila had never forgotten this vow and was determined to fill the role now the time had arrived.

For a few days before the big day, all of the sisters stayed with their father at their aunts' house, sleeping in beds and on sofas, cushions and floors. The excitement was palpable. Mary didn't have enough clothing coupons to buy a wedding gown but she did manage to find a pretty turquoise dress and a short, off-white jacket which she thought would serve well enough. A wartime wedding required all kinds of compromise, after all.

However, two nights before the big day, the Jarmans were sheltering from the bombs in an Underground station and Mary was talking about her forthcoming wedding when, to her surprise, one of her friends from Bermondsey, Julie Burbage, said, 'You can borrow my wedding dress if you like, Mary. But it's a little bit grubby.' Before she could answer, another friend offered to clean the dress for her. Mary couldn't believe her luck, especially when Julie then offered to lend her a bridesmaid dress for Sheila.

Mary and Julie were about the same size, and when she later tried the dress on it fitted her perfectly. However, the bridesmaid dress was not such a good fit for Sheila.

'It's too short, Sheila,' Mary told her. 'I think it would fit Kath well, though.'

Sheila's face dropped. 'You promised me, Mary,' she said. 'The dress is fine.'

Mary sighed. 'OK,' she said, unwilling to shatter Sheila's dreams. 'I suppose it will do.'

Sheila looked at herself in the mirror; the dress ended six inches above her maroon suede shoes. Even if it was a bit short, she thought to herself, she still looked beautiful.

The wedding was a low-key wartime affair with just immediate family and a few friends in attendance. Frank's best man was his army pal, Freddie Becker. The convent venue was rather small but Mary walked the length of it proudly on Pierce's arm to join Frank, dressed in his army uniform, and exchange vows in front of Father Spillane. A glum Pierce looked on, but even her father's subdued spirits couldn't dampen Mary's joy.

The reception was held back at the aunts' house, in what they grandly called the parlour. It was a squeeze and, although there was no money for a wedding cake, there was a spread of cold meat, salad and boiled potatoes, which seemed like a feast to the girls, for whom wartime rations were the norm. After some singing and dancing, the night ended with Mary and Frank sleeping on the couch; Mary's friend Nelly Taylor in one armchair, Freddie Becker in the other; and another of Frank's army pals, Tim Miles, on the floor. It was not a conventional wedding night but Mary had enjoyed the day, and felt happy and relieved that they had managed to marry. Now she was Mrs Marshall and it felt strange to no longer be a Jarman. It was a new chapter.

The following day, the newlyweds set off for their honeymoon – at Frank's sister's house in Oakamoor. There, once more, they spent much of their days going for long walks, but Mary felt that even the most mundane activities or chores were extra special now that they were married. She tried her best to put thoughts of Frank fighting overseas out of her head. This was their time, and she was going to enjoy every second of it.

After a week in Oakamoor, the happy couple returned to Hailsham – Frank back to the army and Mary to Highlands Farm. It seemed like business as usual. However, just a couple of months later, Mary discovered she was pregnant. She was overjoyed. She had always wanted a baby and looked forward to being a loving mother. Frank, too, was delighted when she told him. Their happiness was soon clouded, though, because Frank also had some news. And his sent a shiver through her body.

CHAPTER 9

D-Day, Doodlebugs . . . and Delivery

Aunt Mary (left) with Mary.

'WE'RE SHIPPING OUT,' Frank said calmly, though he felt anything but calm. He and Mary were taking their customary evening stroll through the rec and had just reached the bandstand. Mary's beaming smile evaporated in an instant, excitement replaced by anxiety. 'To France. At the end of the week.'

They had spent precious few private moments together since returning from honeymoon, with Mary feeling more like a Jarman sister again than a wife as she went back to the bedroom she shared with Joan. Frank, meanwhile, practised army manoeuvres by day and slept in the army camp at night. She consoled herself with the thought that nothing much about this marriage was normal. Everything seemed to be happening at a whirlwind pace.

Frank had no choice but to leave his new bride and unborn baby behind as the Canadian troops headed off for the invasion of Normandy, part of a bold Allied task force which hoped to liberate France and northwestern Europe from Nazi control.

Nearly 160,000 troops had already crossed the English Channel on 6 June, as part of Operation Overlord, which became commonly known as D-Day. The amphibious assault, involving more than 5,000 vessels, followed an earlier aerial bombing of German shoreline defences. Five beaches were marked out for the Allied landing, and all were given codenames. The Americans took Utah and Omaha in the west, the British took Gold and Sword in the east, and the Canadians took Juno, in the middle.

For the 14,000 Canadian troops, the journey across the Channel had been full of apprehension, which had turned to blind terror as they stormed ashore and were met by German gunfire and concealed land mines.

News of the D-Day landings on 6 June had thrilled those on the home front, with reports of how the Germans were being pushed back from the Channel shared excitedly from household to household.

'We've got them on the run,' said Pierce, reading his newspaper in the armchair at Battle Road.

The British press had splashed stirring headlines in their D-Day reports: 'Our Armies in N. France', 'The Invasion Has Begun', 'British and Canadians Secure 2 Beachheads' and 'Allied Invasion Troops Several Miles Into France'. However, what was not reported immediately was the human cost of this mission. The initial aerial bombing of the coastline had had no real impact and, as Allied troops waded ashore, chest-high through the water, they were like sitting ducks for the German soldiers nestling in the banks. The Germans razed the shore below with machine-gun fire, causing the invading force to run for cover along sand dotted with land mines. It's estimated that 2,500 Allied soldiers were killed on D-Day, including 340 Canadians. Many more were injured.

Frank was fortunate enough not to be part of this initial wave but now, a few days later, it was his turn.

'I warned you,' Pierce told Mary when he found her moping about the house in the days before Frank's departure. However, Mary didn't want to discuss the issue of her marriage or impending motherhood with her father any more. She suspected that he was so protective towards his daughters that he wouldn't want them marrying *anyone*. What she needed was someone to solve her problems, not add to them. Mary tried to see Frank as much as she could before he left. The day was fast approaching, though, and she was dreading it.

Feeling particularly vulnerable, she took the opportunity to stop working at the farm. True enough, she would have needed to ease back on the work rate later in her pregnancy in any case – the daily milk round saw her work every day, including Sundays, bank holidays and at Christmas and the New Year. However, Mary's urgency to stop work was, in fact, due to her fear of rats.

She was working with another Land Army girl called Helen Saunders, who had also married a Canadian from Frank's regiment, when she heard a voice from the outside toilet saying, 'Shoo! Scram!'

Mary ran over and asked, 'What's wrong?'

'Mary!' Helen answered from inside. 'There's a rat on the floor in front of me.'

'What's it doing?' asked a horrified Mary.

'It's just sitting there . . . watching me.'

Although Helen was more amused than scared, Mary was petrified. It was the final straw; she couldn't put up with the conditions a moment longer. She'd also heard an old wives' tale that if a pregnant woman was scared by a rat, her baby would bear a birthmark in the shape of the rodent. Although Mary didn't truly believe it, she was taking no chances. She promptly asked to be released from her job, admitting to Mr Willoughby, 'I can't stay here any longer – I'm frightened.'

Mary had the chance to say a final goodbye to her new husband the night before he was due to depart for France.

'I'll write to you when I can,' he said to her on the doorstep of 18 Battle Road, after a subdued evening spent mostly in pensive silence. 'Take care of that baby now,' he added, placing a hand on Mary's tummy.

She gave a little smile, trying to hide her worry and sadness from him.

'You take care too, Frank, do you hear?' she replied, her eyes brimming with tears. 'And don't do anything silly.'

Frank smiled. 'What do you mean?' he asked.

Mary gave a heavy sigh. 'I need you,' she faltered. 'In one piece.' She looked down at her growing tummy. 'And our baby does, too,' she added.

Despite his cheery good nature and carefree attitude to life, Frank had become increasingly apprehensive as the days had counted down to the army's departure. He had tried to hide his worry, for Mary's sake, as much as his own, but looking at Mary now, for what might be the last time, he felt a lump in his throat.

'I'll be back before you know it,' he said, and they shared one more lingering kiss before he walked away, wondering what fate lay in store for him on foreign shores.

This second wave of troops, including Frank's regiment, also faced fierce opposition from German soldiers as they pushed ahead after landing, heading for the Norman city of Caen. Generals Montgomery and Eisenhower expected that British, American and Canadian forces would be in control of Normandy and heading east across France within weeks. However, fierce fighting was to take place throughout the summer and Frank would find himself in the thick of it.

Mary and all the women left behind carried on as normal in blissful ignorance. Nevertheless, she had moments when she felt physically sick, wondering if Frank would return or become yet another casualty of the war. She had heard about the nickname that telegram boys had acquired – 'angels of death' – because they usually only arrived to inform women that their husbands or sons were missing or killed in action. The thought of seeing such a messenger on her doorstep sent a shudder through her body and her hands went to her belly instinctively.

In the days following Frank's departure and despite the reported success of the D-Day landings, there had been another terrifying menace on the home front.

Early in the morning of 13 June, just a few days before she was due to give up work, Mary was making her way to Highlands Farm when she had heard an odd sound above her. The 'pop-pop' noise was reminiscent of the stuttering of the small engine of a motorbike. The sky was still quite dark and, peering up through the gloom, she saw what looked like an aircraft with a flame coming from its tail.

'Some poor pilot is in trouble,' she thought to herself as the plane continued on its noisy way.

It wasn't until she listened to the wireless the following day that she learnt she had witnessed the first arrival of an innovative new German weapon, heading towards London and designed to bring terror and destruction.

German scientists had been developing a top-secret *Wunderwaffe*, or 'wonder weapon', and Hitler was determined to use it as quickly as possible, convinced that it would once more turn the tide of the war his way. So, in a show of strength and retaliation for the Allied troops invading Normandy, Hitler boldly initiated the V-1 rocket – short for

Vergeltungswaffen, and meaning 'retaliatory or reprisal weapons'. Launched from the French coastline stretching between Calais and Boulogne, and also from the Dutch coast further north, the V-1 targeted London. Three years after the terror of the Blitz, Londoners who had thought that they were now comparatively safe on the home front, were being terrorized once more.

These flying bombs were pilotless and powered by a pulsejet engine that gave them a characteristic buzzing sound and earned them the nickname doodlebugs. The bombs were fitted with a device that cut the engine when it was estimated to have reached its target area. That silence was one Londoners soon learnt to dread because it meant the bomb was about to drop. Many would count to ten and then wait for the explosion.

What Mary had seen in the dark sky in Hailsham, mistaking it for a plane on fire, was the characteristic flame that came from the tailpipe of all V-1s. Thousands more of these doodlebugs headed for London over the coming months, but not all of them reached the capital. Many fell far short of their target destination and others were shot down by the RAF, which meant the Jarman girls, too, feared the sound, like so many others.

The first of the V-1s, which Mary had seen and heard, landed at Swanscombe in Kent, just short of the all-important Tilbury Docks. The second, launched shortly afterwards, came down in Cuckfield, to the west of Haywards Heath in West Sussex. With the RAF busily deployed either trying to shoot down the rockets or deflect them off target, many came down in Sussex and Kent. Country life became rather more perilous.

At school, Sheila couldn't concentrate when she heard

doodlebugs approaching, praying that her daddy would be safe back in London, and praying too that the bombs didn't come down early. If they flew over when she was outside, she would duck down behind the nearest hedge, despite the futility of it offering any protection should the bomb fall. Indoors, the girls took once more to cowering in the Morrison shelter whenever they heard the dreaded buzzing sound, which was happening increasingly often.

A group of pupils at Hailsham Senior Mixed School were outside tending the vegetable patch one afternoon when an air-raid siren sounded. Above the noise, they could still make out the drone of a doodlebug flying overhead. A few moments later, to their horror, the engine cut out.

'Take cover!' yelled the teacher, Mr Taylor.

With little time to go anywhere, they crouched by a wall, arms covering their heads . . . and waited. However, the next sound they heard was not the expected explosion but the engine of a plane. As they peered up apprehensively, they saw a British Typhoon fighter delicately place its own wing under the wing of the rocket. The fighter guided the rocket away so that it dropped and exploded in open fields a few miles from the school. It was a remarkable display of aviation and the children talked about nothing else for weeks. The manoeuvre became a frequent sight in various parts of the South of England, though, as RAF planes tried to guide the bombs off course from London and the surrounding populated areas to explode in safer places.

Despite these renewed aerial threats over Britain, the war in Europe was slowly turning in favour of the Allies. French and Italian cities were liberated during the long summer of 1944, while in the East, the Russians were re-taking their land from the Germans. As the summer wore on, the mood became remarkably optimistic.

Now that the Canadian and American soldiers were no longer in and around Hailsham, things seemed oddly quiet. Joan, now seventeen, was missing the pleasant distraction that they provided away from the drudge of 'motherhood'.

'It just seems so quiet and, well, boring here without them,' she said to Mary as they were preparing a meal in the kitchen. 'I only ever leave the house to go to the shops.'

Neither of them knew how things were about to change.

Sheila had left school at fourteen and started work at Green Brothers factory. She wondered what her mother's reaction would have been to her working there, after the confrontation with the foreman years earlier. However, unlike Mary, she wasn't having to sew smelly and dirty sacks, and, besides, there wasn't a great deal of choice when it came to local work.

In conversation at home, Sheila mentioned that the company was looking for part-time staff to make ropes for warships. Joan's ears pricked up but she said nothing to her sister. Instead, the next day, she went down to Greens to enquire about the job, and walked away as a part-time employee. She had mentioned the fact that her sister Sheila worked there but, like Sheila, had made no mention of Mary's one-morning stint and their mother's tirade!

The work didn't prove to be as bad as Mary's had been but it was still quite unpleasant, coiling lengths of heavy rope that trailed on damp, stone floors, that then became very dirty. However, it was only for four hours a day and

Joan welcomed the break from the house. With Mary having given up work during her pregnancy and being able to look after Anne when she wasn't at nursery or with Rosie Goldsmith, it also brought in some much-needed extra money.

Despite Annie's opinion of working at Greens years earlier, both of the girls were sure that their mother would have approved of their jobs. They were doing what being a family and pulling together was all about. Annie, having struggled financially all her life, knew the value of money all too well and she was always grateful for any extra income. As Greens was just a short walk away from Battle Road there were no travel expenses either.

Back when they had lived in Bermondsey, things had definitely been tougher in some ways. Just having enough money for the bus fare to work at Koupy Gowns had been a frequent trial for Mary. After giving Annie her weekly 12 shillings wage and being handed back 2 shillings, Mary's money didn't go very far. Although Mary never resented it and had been pleased to be able to help her mother and support her sisters, it had meant that she was often unable to pay her bus fare to and from work. Annie would hand Mary her daily fare but by Friday, or even by Thursday, the ten shillings would have been eaten up and Annie would desperately be searching for coins to cover Mary's travel costs.

Not wanting to embarrass her mother, Mary occasionally went downstairs and asked her uncle Mike if he would let her have some money so that she could get to work. Mike had problems with reading and writing, and had never gone out to work, so his parents used to give him some money from time to time when he did various chores. The family might not have considered him capable of being able to look after himself but he had a mind for money. He also showed a rare flair for the horses and his weekly bet on the races invariably saw him picking up winnings from the local bookie.

Mary hated having to ask Mike for her bus fare, though, because he was always very reluctant to part with his money. He wouldn't say much. In fact, he rarely said anything at all. There was usually a lengthy silence before he eventually mumbled, 'I'm short myself,' or 'Can't your mum help you out?'

In the end he had always given in and handed her the money, but not before he had made her late for work.

'Thanks, Uncle Mike,' she would say quickly and then rush out the door before she missed another bus.

With Joan able to walk to work at Greens, everything felt easier to manage and the two young women settled into a routine quickly. Joan felt useful again and Mary was enjoying looking after Anne, getting in some parenting practice before her own baby arrived.

Having heard the glowing reports of the success of the D-Day landings on the wireless, but nothing of the Allied casualty toll, Mary didn't feel overly worried about Frank being in the midst of it. Nevertheless, after he'd been away for six weeks she was relieved and delighted to receive a letter from him, saying that he was well and that he missed her, and that he hoped they would be reunited soon. He made no mention of his terrifying ordeal, the many lives that had been lost, or the continuing life-threatening danger he was in as the Allied troops pushed deeper into France in the offensive against Germany.

D-Day, Doodlebugs . . . and Delivery

A long summer of fighting against the Germans ensued before the Allies finally managed to break out of Normandy and, in August, a pincer movement of Canadian, British, Polish and American forces cut off the retreat of the German Army through the town of Falaise, inland from Caen. The Normandy campaign finally ended on 21 August and the pursuit of the enemy into Holland, Belgium and Germany itself was now on.

Germany was now on the back foot and many of Hitler's top generals despaired of his increasingly defiant insistence to attack at all costs – even when retreat would have saved the lives of tens of thousands of German soldiers. However, in spite of this, the Führer decided to attack Britain on the home front once again. This time with a new, improved version of the V-1.

The V-2 rocket was an astonishing advance in technology. The V-1 had caused terror with its distinctive sound that warned of its arrival and potentially imminent explosion, whereas the V-2 travelled faster than the speed of sound, crashing and exploding without warning, bringing with it a different kind of terror. The first V-2 was launched towards Paris on 8 September 1944, and caused modest damage near Porte d'Italie. This was followed by another V-2 attack on London on the same day. The bomb landed in Chiswick, West London, reducing rows of houses to rubble, killing three people and seriously injuring seventeen.

These frightening weapons caused the Jarman sisters to be even more concerned about their father. During the evenings, Pierce had taken on air-raid duties in Bermondsey, walking the streets to make sure that all lights were out during bombing raids and guiding people to shelters. He was also part of the night-time fire-watch team, based on top of the town hall near to where he worked. If the team saw any building set on fire by a bomb they would telephone the National Fire Service, but tackled smaller fires themselves.

There was ample opportunity for Pierce to be affected by Hitler's new weapon and the girls worried about him all the time. At night, in their beds in Battle Road, the girls would pray to God for the safety of their father as well as Frank.

In the midst of this hell, at times life carried on in a very normal way for the girls. In stark contrast to dark and dangerous war-battered London, Kath and Pat got to wear their pretty white Communion dresses once more, when they made their Confirmation. This sacrament – a confirmation of the vows made during the Baptism service – took place in neighbouring Eastbourne. The journey was as exciting as the event itself because Father Frost drove them there in his car, along with a couple of other girls from their school. Kath and Pat had never been in a car before and they felt like princesses being chauffeured to a ball. More delights came after the official service when they were treated to tea, cake and soft drinks in beautiful tea gardens at Wannock, just outside Polegate. Here the girls looked in wonder at the lily ponds, rock garden and, in one of the greenhouses, a delightful miniature Japanese garden.

'Mind you don't drop anything down your dress, Pat,' Kath cautioned her younger sister, as both bit into a slice of cake. They enjoyed this part of the day much more than the church service. The weather was beautifully sunny, birds sang in the garden, and war, deprivation and sadness were bleached from their consciousness for a brief but blissful period as they lifted their smiling faces up to the warming sun. Even when it was time to go back home, they looked forward to getting into the car once more with Father Frost. This small but golden memory stayed with the two girls for the rest of their lives.

Christmas 1944 saw people in better spirits than they had been in years. Finally, it really did look like this dreadful war, which seemed to have gone on and on with raised hopes and dashed expectations, might soon end. Paris had been liberated by the Allies on 25 August and German troops in the French ports of Boulogne-sur-Mer and Calais had surrendered at the end of September.

The prospect of peace, however, took another battering when Hitler surprised the Allies once more with a major offensive a week before Christmas. American units in northwest Europe were caught off guard when German tanks and troops thrust through the Ardennes, heading for the Belgian port of Antwerp. The bold move aimed to split the Allied line allowing the Germans to encircle and destroy them. As the Germans drove deeper through the forest, the Allied line, as depicted on maps, took on the appearance of a large bulge and gave rise to the offensive's name, the Battle of the Bulge.

Christmas in Hailsham saw Mary heavily pregnant with her baby. For her monthly antenatal check-ups she had been given the opportunity to go either to the hospital in Eastbourne or to Guy's Hospital, by London Bridge, which was the closest hospital to their Abbey Street home. Mary had thought she wanted to be at Guy's, as it was one of the biggest and most renowned hospitals in the country. However, she began to regret her decision when the monthly journeys to London became an increasing ordeal.

In mid-January 1945, three weeks before she was due to give birth, Guy's Hospital arranged for Mary to move to Northampton, safely away from the V-2 rockets both in the capital and along the south coast. There she would stay at a house with two other young women, also pregnant for the first time. When the time came to give birth, they would be admitted to the local hospital. What should have made life easier turned into one of the worst experiences of her life and, although she was only at the house for a few weeks, it seemed an eternity.

The elderly landlady was completely insensitive to the feelings of apprehension the young women were experiencing. All were just twenty years old, anxious about pregnancy and giving birth, particularly as they were away from their husbands, families and friends.

On top of this, conditions inside the house were spartan. Mary had to share a double bed with one of the expectant mums, Maudie, who lived in the Old Kent Road, while the other had a single bed in a separate bedroom. It was freezing cold outside, where the snow lay ten inches thick, and inside the house it wasn't much warmer. Each night, the three women had to share one hot water bottle between them to warm their beds – not easy when one of them was sleeping in another bedroom. On one night, the bottle would start in the double bed, warming it before the women got in, and then it would be passed to the single bed for the rest of the night. The following night, the procedure would be swapped so the bottle warmed the single bed first.

'I'm not sure who's the luckiest,' said Mary to Maudie

one night after the water bottle was removed from their bed. 'Having the water bottle while it's really hot or getting it not so hot but being able to put your feet on it until it goes cold . . .'

The landlady didn't believe in the women sitting or lying around all day. She stressed that exercise was healthy and vital, and terrified them by saying, 'If you don't get enough exercise your baby will stick to your womb.'

Not knowing anything about such matters, they firmly believed her and so walked with her every day, through the snow, into the centre of Northampton. It was while they were in town that they visited the chemist to purchase a razor and toilet paper, which they had been asked to supply for themselves during their stay in hospital. Embarrassed about buying these personal items, they pretended to the shop assistant that they were parcelling them up to send to their husbands on the war front.

One evening at dinner, Maudie was having trouble chewing and swallowing the fatty meat on her plate. After doing her best, she ended up leaving most of it.

'Why haven't you eaten your meat, Maudie?' the landlady asked, clearly unhappy.

Maudie didn't want to hurt her feelings by telling her that it was fatty. Besides, she was too frightened to complain, so she answered, 'I'm not very keen on meat, to be honest.'

The landlady said nothing but raised her eyebrows. The remark was noted and Maudie came to regret her little lie because she wasn't given any more meat at all during her stay and often felt hungry. All three of the women thought that the landlady disapproved of them being young mothers, and that was why she treated them like naughty, foolish schoolchildren rather than women who were about to become parents.

How Mary wished she had gone to Eastbourne Hospital, where she could still see her father and her sisters, who she missed desperately. Northampton was just too far away for them to visit. The isolation was miserable and she clung on to the idea of her baby – it wouldn't be long now before it arrived.

When Mary's contractions started late in the evening, the landlady insisted that she make the journey to hospital by foot, instead of calling for an ambulance.

'The walk will do you good,' she insisted.

The snow was still thick so Mary put on her wellies and trudged alongside her landlady in the dark to the hospital, a fifteen-minute walk away. However, it took much longer because Mary had to keep stopping to catch her breath, and it was while she was holding on to some railings that surrounded a US Army base, halfway through the journey, that her waters broke.

'Something's happened,' said a horrified Mary, as she felt the wetness running down her legs and into her wellies. 'I'm soaking wet!'

'Your waters have broken,' said the landlady, as matter of fact as ever. 'Come on, let's get a move on. The quicker we walk, the quicker we'll be at the hospital.'

The rest of the journey was even more horrendous. Mary felt the American soldiers could probably hear her squelching past their base! It was a great relief when the hospital finally came into sight. Once there, she was taken into the delivery room, clutching her razor and toilet paper, and spent sixteen hours in labour, wearing long white compression stockings to prevent blood clots, and feeling absolutely terrified.

Unfortunately the midwife, like Mary's landlady, was lacking in compassion. After giving her some gas and air she took a no-nonsense approach to the proceedings. 'Now push,' she shouted at her young charge. 'And pant.'

Mary was clueless and the midwife rebuked her sharply whenever she didn't do as she was told. It was a lot to take in. And then there was the pain . . . She just hadn't been prepared for this. She had had no mother to talk to about such things; Pierce hadn't been able to help. How she longed to have her mother by her side. Right now, she felt like she needed Annie more than ever.

Annie, after all, had given birth six times, so would have been able to tell her exactly what to expect and put her mind at ease. It was the fear of the unknown that was so traumatic. During this difficult time she imagined how wonderful it would be to have her mother by her side, smiling and holding her hand.

Finally, Mary gave birth at 2 p.m. on 7 February 1945 to a baby boy whom she named Christopher. She remained in hospital for fourteen days, as was usual at the time. For the first week she was confined to bed and wasn't even allowed to sit up. She had to eat all her meals lying on her side and had no visitors. However, Mary felt she could bear anything now. She was relieved and delighted to have given birth safely to a baby boy. Her only wish was that Frank could be there to see him.

After two weeks, Aunt Nell arrived to accompany Mary and her new baby back to Hailsham. After all that time lying in a hospital bed with no exercise, Mary felt weak and thought her legs looked terribly thin. Nell was her usual matter-of-fact self and didn't even smile at the baby or Mary. She was no substitute for Annie but Mary hadn't expected her to make a fuss, and so she wasn't disappointed. Just saddened. In contrast, her sisters were delighted and excited to see baby Christopher, their first nephew. Even Pierce gingerly held his grandson in his arms. Mary was greatly comforted by being at home with her family after what she could only describe as an ordeal.

On the war front, the Battle of the Bulge had come to a quick end on 28 January as the Allies, having recovered from the surprise, used their superior numbers to push the Germans back decisively. Now they were retreating into Germany itself.

However, whilst Mary was feeling safe and comforted within the bosom of her family, V-2 rockets were still flying over and falling, for the most part, on London. Then, on the night of Friday 2 March, a strike on Dockhead shocked the Jarman family, along with the rest of the strong Catholic community of that part of Bermondsey.

Pierce had already left for Hailsham, as usual, shortly after finishing work, but later that evening, just before 11 p.m., a V-2 rocket hit the presbytery near Most Holy Trinity Church, causing the four-storey building to collapse. Three priests – Stephen Spillane, who had married Mary and Frank, Finbar MacCarthy and Michael O'Riordan – were all killed instantly. A fourth, Edmund Arbuthnott, along with the housekeeper, Bridget Slavin, miraculously survived.

Father Arbuthnott had been trapped beneath rubble and thought he was likely to die. Having passed out temporarily after the bomb hit, he had awoken on the floor with a mass of debris pinning him down. Local people had rushed to the scene but there seemed little hope of finding anyone alive. However, when a rescue party from the local Civil Defence Service arrived, milkman turned section leader Albert 'Ted' Heming had heard a faint cry for help. He crawled through a small hole and painstakingly removed the bricks, rubble and a main timber that was pinning Father Arbuthnott down. Despite the danger of further rubble falling and burying them both, the priest was rescued after three hours and taken to hospital, along with Bridget Slavin, where they both made a full recovery.

The relationship between parishioners and their priests in Dockhead had never been confined to weekly mass attendance. The priests would regularly visit their parishioners' homes and were held in high esteem by the congregation. They were also the people that parishioners could go to for help.

Shortly before the war, Annie had sought help from the then parish priest, Father O'Kane, when she couldn't afford the money needed for Mary to go on a two-week school trip to the Isle of Wight. Knowing how much Mary wanted to go, and desperately wishing she had the money but not wanting to increase her debt with the pawnbroker, she had turned to the priest. He had agreed to lend her the money and she had duly paid it back in instalments without any crippling interest. Even her brother Mike would have charged her interest if she'd borrowed money from him!

A delighted Mary, who had no idea how her mother had afforded it, went to Portsmouth excitedly, with twenty other girls and two teachers, to board the boat to the Isle of Wight. Had she known, Annie might have saved herself the embarrassment of having to ask her priest for money because, once there, Mary couldn't wait to come home! The party were staying at a convent in Shanklin and Mary enjoyed herself well enough for the first few days, but then unfortunately became terribly homesick and couldn't stop crying. All the other girls were having so much fun they couldn't understand why Mary was so upset.

'I just want to go home,' she kept saying.

There would be no christening for Christopher in Dockhead, then, but it was playing on Pierce's mind that his grandson still hadn't received the first sacrament.

'When are you going to get that baby christened?' he asked Mary, and not for the first time.

Despite the disruption to their lives, Pierce still liked to be religious-minded when it came to his daughters' upbringing, and continued to make sure they were all up in time for Sunday morning mass each week, just as Annie had done, despite his own reluctance to set foot inside the church.

'I'm waiting for Frank,' Mary replied. 'He may be getting leave soon.'

'Well, you can't wait for ever,' said Pierce, privately wondering whether she would ever see Frank again.

'Things seem to be going well,' said a resilient Mary. 'Who knows? It might soon be over.'

Eventually, feeling she could wait no longer for Frank's return, Mary went ahead with the christening. However, just two weeks later Frank did return to Hailsham on leave. There was a joyful reunion with Mary and he was finally able to meet two-month-old baby Christopher, who, in the midst of war, he had worried he might never see.

Frank never told Mary much about his experiences in the heat of the battle. Like many soldiers, he felt that the horrors of war couldn't be described adequately to those who hadn't experienced them, and so it was best to avoid such details. Now, holding Chris in his arms and walking as a family in the rec, fighting in France seemed unreal. He was due to return there in a week's time, but by then everyone understood that the end of the war was very much in sight. Before he departed, he and Mary discussed their future.

'You'd like Canada,' Frank said to his wife. 'The space and the trees, the landscape . . . It'll take your breath away.'

Mary, whose only trip off the mainland had been that ill-fated school journey by ferry to the Isle of Wight, was fascinated and keen to experience Canada but didn't want to live there permanently because she knew she would miss her family. She could hardly contemplate being without her sisters and Pierce, but at the same time she had so much to look forward to now that she had a family of her own.

'I'd like to see it, Frank,' she said. 'But I wouldn't want to live there for ever.'

'It's entirely up to you,' he replied. 'Come out and we'll live with my parents in Calgary, and if you don't like it, then we'll come back and live in England. How's that sound?'

Mary smiled. 'Promise?'

'Promise,' he confirmed.

Shortly after Frank returned to France, those words, 'it might soon be over', said by so many throughout the various phases of the war, finally became an accurate assessment. In the final push, the Western Allies raced the Russians to be the first into Berlin. The Russians won, entering the German capital on 21 April 1945. Hitler committed suicide nine days later in his bunker and finally, after almost five and a half years of war, Germany made an unconditional surrender on 7 May 1945. It was all over.

The news that the war had ended in Europe was relayed to the British people over the wireless later that day. The nation was informed that the following day would be officially known as Victory in Europe (VE) Day and would be a national holiday. As news came through that German forces had surrendered in Italy and then Holland, Denmark and northwest Germany, many Brits had already started celebrating, knowing already, in the days leading up to the announcement, that the war was ending.

On VE Day, the Jarman family, in common with many others across the nation, were huddled around the wireless at 3 p.m. to listen to Churchill's speech.

> We may allow ourselves a brief period of rejoicing; but let us not forget for a moment the toil and efforts that lie ahead. Japan, with all her treachery and greed, remains unsubdued. The injury she has inflicted on Great Britain, the United States, and other countries, and her detestable cruelties, call for justice and retribution. We must now devote all our strength and resources to the completion of our task, both at home and abroad. Advance, Britannia! Long live the cause of freedom! God save the King!

In 18 Battle Road, the girls cheered and danced. Nobody more so than Sheila. It would mean they could go home to Bermondsey at long last. However, a moment later she remembered that they no longer had a home to go to.

Later on, the prime minister appeared on the balcony of the Ministry of Health building in central London and gave an impromptu speech to the cheering crowds below, declaring, 'This is your victory.'

People seemed almost light-headed with disbelief that the war had finally ended, and there was much singing, dancing and drinking in the streets, which were adorned with Union Jack flags and bunting. King George VI and the Queen appeared eight times on the balcony of Buckingham Palace, while, it was later revealed, the two princesses, Margaret and Elizabeth, slipped out of Buckingham Palace to mingle anonymously with the crowds, enjoying the carnival-like atmosphere up close.

The Jarman girls each began to turn their thoughts to returning to a bomb-ravished London, wondering just what the future held for them.

CHAPTER 10

Farewell, Hailsham

*Photograph of Pierce on his ID card
for the London Electricity Board.*

'THAT'S IT THEN, girls,' said Pierce. 'We're going home.'

A few days after VE Day, he gathered the girls in the kitchen to deliver the news. The Government wouldn't get round to approving the return of evacuees officially until the following month but a great many children were reunited with their families earlier than that. After all, thought the parents, what was the point in waiting now that the war was over?

Pierce's comment was met by silence as each girl contemplated just what 'going home' actually meant. Kath and Pat had spent their formative years in Hailsham, and couldn't remember much else. Their intrepid journey into the unknown over five years ago, against a backdrop of global uncertainty about the future, now seemed like the dim and distant past to girls of such tender years. For all of them, Heywood, 18 Battle Road – the address automatically ringing in their ears to the tune of Sheila's whimsical ditty – now seemed more like home to them than anywhere else.

The thought surprised them, even Joan, who had grown into her role as 'mother'. She was used to it now – the shops, the friends, the kitchen, the routine. Motherhood – the protective nature of it – had come too early into her life, but it was a role that she had accepted and filled remarkably well. What would it mean in Bermondsey? And where would they live? She had also liked having her part-time job at Greens and wondered if she would find similar hours of employment in London.

There was uncertainty for Mary, too. Frank had returned to the army and would be going home to Canada eventually. The thought of joining him there with baby Chris was both exciting and terrifying in equal measure.

To Anne, who had just turned six, returning to London sounded like another adventure. She had heard many stories about Bermondsey. Now, she would be able to experience it for herself. As long as she had her family around her she was happy.

Only Sheila, of all the sisters, felt her spirits lift. Her mother might no longer be with them but moving back to Bermondsey and, more specifically, Dockhead, was the nearest she could get to a return to normality; how things were before this unwelcome and dramatic chapter in their lives had taken place.

'Well?' asked Pierce. 'All happy? It's what we've been waiting for.'

'Where are we going to live?' asked Joan.

'We'll live with my sisters for a while, until we get sorted,' he said, with a hopeful little smile.

The news was not well received by any of the sisters. Even Sheila had a sudden alarming image of them all squeezing into their aunts' double bed!

'How will we be sorted?' Joan asked, ever the practical one.

Pierce was not entirely sure but used a familiar line of Annie's. 'I'll have a word with the council,' he replied.

*

Suitcases and bags were packed with clothes and the few other possessions they had acquired over the years, but they had been instructed to leave behind all of the items that been donated to them. Aunt Rose, who had come down from Bermondsey to accompany the girls back to London, had other ideas.

'They won't want all this back,' she said, piling cutlery, crockery, and pots and pans into bags. Besides, it was given to us.'

Sheila looked at her dubiously but said nothing.

Annie's ploy of telling the kindly Mrs Hassen that they were short of blankets had finally paid off as they now added the extra ones to the things to be taken home. Sheila was in two minds, but even she had to admit that they probably deserved an extra item or two, after all they'd been through.

Lifting Annie's beloved clock from the mantelpiece, Pierce felt misty-eyed as he secured the pendulum to stop its movement – its incessant and familiar ticking silenced at a stroke. Then, he carefully wrapped it in some clothing and nestled it inside his suitcase.

'Just listen to that chime, Pierce. Sounds very regal, doesn't it? I'm sure it will last for years and years.' Her words came echoing into the room.

Extraordinary to think that she had lived there with them, the beating heart of the family, but was gone for ever. He closed the case quickly and walked outside to see if the girls were ready to go.

With everyone carrying something, they trooped out of Heywood, 18 Battle Road and closed the side door for the final time. They never did get to use the front door. They were leaving behind a house that had become a home – one full of dramatic and varied memories – in which they had experienced displacement, death, overwhelming grief, romance, laughter, marriage and new life. There was little time to reminisce on such things, though, because as they were walking along the High Street to the train station, Rose caught sight of Mrs Hassen behind them in the distance, coming their way. Perhaps, Rose thought, she had checked the house and found many of the items missing. The formidable Rose felt unusually nervous.

'Quick! Get a move on!' she urged. 'Mrs Hassen's coming. Don't stop!'

At the station, they spent a fretful few minutes wondering if Mrs Hassen would arrive before their train did. Just as the train pulled in, there she appeared along the platform.

'Hello! Just a minute!' she called out, waving in their direction.

Suspecting that she knew what they were up to – and they certainly had their hands full, that much was clear – Rose called back, 'We've no time! We'll miss the train!'

She ushered everyone aboard quickly and in her haste Joan, who was carrying a pilfered broom, dropped it in the gap between the train and platform.

'Leave it, Joan!' Rose hissed. 'Just get on.'

Mrs Hassen looked on, uncertain what to do as they sat inside the carriage, staring straight ahead, determined not to look at her – except surreptitiously out of the corner of their eyes! To their relief, the station master blew his whistle and the train shuddered into motion. The large metal wheels turned and the train pulled away slowly, leaving a cloud of steam in its wake, which slowly dissipated until there was no trace at all.

Alighting at London Bridge station with various other evacuees, there was a heightened sense of excitement at the familiar hustle and bustle of London. It all came flooding back to the girls. As they walked down the steps into Tooley Street, however, it was immediately evident that Bermondsey had taken a battering over the past several years. Many of the buildings had been damaged by bombs and some had been reduced to nothing more than piles of rubble.

'It looks so drab compared to the countryside, doesn't it?' said Mary, taking in the scene around her.

'Smelly, too,' commented Kath, turning her nose up at the mixture of aromas, from fresh meat and vegetables, to brick dust and goodness knows what else emanating from markets, factories and houses. Already, she was missing the fresh country smells of Hailsham: the rec, the fields and woodland nature trails. Bermondsey no longer seemed like home.

At their aunts' house in Stanworth Street they unpacked their belongings as Nell and Mary looked approvingly at the crockery, cutlery and blankets.

'We had a lovely broom, too,' Rose told her sisters, glancing crossly at Joan. 'But Joan dropped it on the railway track.'

'Couldn't someone get it for you?' asked Nell.

'We were in a bit of a rush,' Mary interjected.

'That busybody Mrs Hassen,' added Rose. 'Chasing after us like that. Checking up on us. It's none of her business.'

'She was very kind to us, Aunt,' said Joan, feeling sorry

that Mrs Hassen was being maligned despite all she had done to help the family during their stay.

Rose shook her head and pursed her lips. 'Nosy, that's what she was. Now then. Let's get things put away. Everyone needs to help out.'

Later, the aunts treated the girls to some coconut cake, with the obligatory slice of bread and butter to aid digestion. When it was time for the afternoon nap, Joan suggested that she and her sisters go for a walk instead, so that the aunts could have some peace and quiet from having too many people in the house. To the girls' relief the aunts agreed and the Jarman sisters trooped along familiar yet somehow unfamiliar streets – a consequence of time clouding memory and Luftwaffe bombs having altered the local landscape.

Abbey Street had been particularly badly hit, with many buildings now razed to the ground. They stopped opposite their own home to take in the sorry sight of the badly damaged house. The splendid Virginia creeper that had covered the front and made it stand out against neighbouring houses, adding colour and life, much to Annie's pleasure; the sunflowers in the back yard that their granddad had grown, and the elderberry tree that was the source of Mrs Bradley's home-made wine; the half-moon outside the door that Annie would scrub on the paving stone . . . All gone. Their house-proud mother's constant cleaning inside, and their own regular household chores, her prized three-piece suite. What would she have thought if she could see how it had ended up?

Later that evening, back at their aunts' house, the girls were reunited with their father after he had finished work and, over dinner, they discussed their future.

Farewell, Hailsham

'The council has been looking at a few possible places for us to live,' said Pierce.

'Will it be far from here, Daddy?' asked Anne. Pierce gave her a little smile.

'No, not far,' he replied. 'We're back now.'

They were all keen to get settled in their own house as quickly as possible. It was too much of a squeeze living with the aunts. Pierce had his own little bedroom and the aunts their double bed. There was a third bedroom for Mary and baby Chris but the rest of the girls had an ad hoc sleeping arrangement utilizing sofas, armchairs and cushions in the living room. Each of them declined the offer of squeezing into the aunts' bed! It was evident to everyone that the quicker the council found them a home, the better.

Kath and Pat soon went back to school at St Joseph's where they were reunited with old friends, many of whom had also been evacuated for the duration of war, but there were others who had returned home a few years earlier. The sisters settled in to the new rhythms of school life easily enough, but without their realizing it, living in Hailsham had softened their cockney accents, so much so that several of the other children laughed at them and said they talked 'posh'.

Kath was also taken aback in class one day, when she was writing an English composition and wrote about 'my friend' in her story. The girl sitting next to her happened to see what she had written and frowned at her.

'You don't say "my friend",' she declared, appalled at such language. 'You say "my mate".'

Kath felt uncomfortable about this. School life meant

fitting in with your peers. They had managed to do it at Hailsham. Well, mostly. Kath never imagined that she would have to try to modify her behaviour to fit in once more – at her old school. Had she really changed that much? She was surprised to learn that she had.

At school in Hailsham, they had become accustomed to returning to their seat politely if they happened to be standing when anyone, such as another teacher or a priest, walked into the room. It was a simple sign of respect. When Kath did that in St Joseph's, as another nun entered the room, she was again corrected by her classmate.

'What did you do that for?' she was asked.

'You have to,' Kath replied.

'No, you don't! You just carry on with what you're doing.'

Once more, Kath frowned. She didn't like being different or being told she was posh. It was an insult. She had to mend her ways.

Joan carried on looking after Anne and helping with the cooking, shopping and cleaning at the aunts' house, as the family eagerly awaited a house of their own. She was missing her independence working at Greens. It hadn't been a dream job but it had got her out of the house and was a break from the domestic drudgery. Life just became busy without it – a daily bustle of things to do.

In an effort to enjoy some leisure time, Joan persuaded Sheila to join the local social club with her at the church hall. Sheila, who was still shy and felt as if she was almost starting again in Bermondsey, was apprehensive but agreed. However, on their way there on the first evening, Sheila felt anxious all of a sudden.

'I can't go, Joan,' she said, standing stock-still in the street.

'What do you mean?' asked Joan, who was keen to get out of the house and enjoy the company of other young people their age.

'I just can't do it. I'm too nervous.'

'Don't be silly, Sheila. Of course you can. We know lots of people there.'

Sheila felt sick at the idea of walking in as a newcomer. 'I can't do it right now,' she said. 'Another night. But not now.'

Joan sighed and reluctantly started to walk back home with her sister. They had only gone a little way when Joan decided to have one more attempt at persuasion. 'You know, if you don't go now, then you won't go at all,' she said. 'You'll just find an excuse to put it off each time.'

Sheila thought about this for a few moments and then stopped in her tracks once more.

'OK,' she said. 'Come on. Let's do it.'

They turned and made their way to the club, arm in arm. To their delight, some of the Eddicott girls were there, and so too was Joan's good friend from before the war, Lena Sullivan, who rushed over to Joan and embraced her warmly. For the first time, it really felt like coming home.

Sheila was pleased she had done it. Settling back in to life in Bermondsey and their old community was now firmly underway, and she now had the confidence to find herself a job as a machinist in Beak Street, in the West End.

As the rest of the girls all settled in during the first three weeks of their return, Mary was on tenterhooks. She was awaiting the date of her passage to Canada to be reunited with Frank. And Pierce was dreading the day that would happen. His daughters had stuck together through peace and war, they'd always understood the importance of family and how lucky they were to have each other, and he couldn't bear the thought of any of them leaving. Losing Mary would be a huge blow. He tried to take his mind off the thought as much as he could by focusing on the pressing concern of moving out of his sisters' house and into a home of their own.

'Is there anything available in Thorburn Square?' Pierce asked the housing officer during another visit to the council offices. He recalled Annie saying how much she had admired the big houses there. It was situated between Southwark Park Road – The Blue – and Rolls Road, and Annie had always slowed down to look at the homes there whenever they'd been passing.

The officer adjusted his spectacles and peered at the papers held together in a large cardboard file. 'Not in the Square itself but we do have some houses in that area,' he replied. 'There's one, two, three . . . six houses we could show you.'

Pierce smiled. He felt Annie looking down, urging him to do her proud. 'Don't let them fob you off,' he could hear her saying. He was determined to get the best possible home for his daughters. After all they'd been through, without fuss and without complaint, he felt they more than deserved it.

An appointment was made to view the available houses, and he immediately felt a surge of optimism and comfort that at long last they could start living together properly as a family, albeit without Annie. He felt that he couldn't make the decision of choosing a house without his daughters' help, though, and so all of them – including six-year-old Anne – accompanied him and the housing officer as they visited six properties in the area surrounding Thorburn Square.

Farewell, Hailsham

There was less bomb damage there than in Abbey Street and the buildings were largely intact. It was almost as if the war hadn't happened. Mary smiled to herself as they trooped from house to house, recalling how, when they were small, Annie would take them shopping down The Blue. She often used to make them take the long route home, walking through Thorburn Square and along neighbouring Lynton Road, simply so that she could admire the smart, red-brick Victorian houses. So, when they viewed an attractive-looking two-storey house in Lynton Road, which had three bedrooms, a sitting room, dining room, kitchen and small garden, Mary, Joan and Sheila all urged their father to choose it.

A few days later, Pierce and the girls packed their meagre belongings to start a new life together – no longer in Abbey Street or Battle Road but in Lynton Road. Each one of them knew how happy it would have made their mother that they were all safely back together, living in a house that she would have approved of. So long as they kept it clean!

Epilogue

The Jarman sisters, 1995 (from left to right) Joan, Anne, Ruth, Sheila, Mary and Pat.

AFTER VICTORY IN Europe, the people of Britain returned to a peaceful life. The conflict that was ongoing in the Far East came to a drastic and devastating end when the world's first atomic bomb was dropped on the Japanese city of Hiroshima on 6 August 1945, followed by another on Nagasaki three days later. These terrifying weapons led to the surrender of Japan on 14 August, bringing the Second World War to an end.

Peace might have been restored, however, the hardship felt, particularly by struggling working-class families such as the Jarmans, continued as rationing went on for another decade.

The Jarmans' strong bond, strengthened during their evacuation years, continued to thrive in Lynton Road as they lived together and shared their experiences – romance, tragedy, hardship and good times – until, one by one, they moved away.

Kath left school at the age of fourteen and got a job as a dressmaker in the West End's Cavendish Square, and Shelia left her machinist job to work in the Peek Frean biscuit factory in Bermondsey. With Anne joining Pat at St Joseph's, Joan continued in her housewife role, but missed the countryside of Hailsham and working at Greens. Then, one day she surprised everyone by announcing that she had got herself a job as personnel assistant at a local fur and leather manufacturing company, named Alaska. She enjoyed going out to earn money for herself, despite still doing most of the housework at home.

Mary, who so longed to join Frank in Canada, finally got her notice to sail aboard the RMS *Queen Mary* in June 1946. As she prepared to make the long journey with sixteen-month-old Chris, never in her wildest dreams could she have imagined what lay in store for her.

Acknowledgements

To the Jarman sisters, whose stories of their childhood evacuation have been passed down the family over the generations. Thanks for answering my many questions and for the use of photographs, the supplying of tea and for coping admirably with lights, camera, action.

Mary's memoirs, compiled by her eldest daughter Anne, helped inspire this book and proved to be invaluable. The family genealogy that my cousin Richard (Anne, the youngest Jarman sister's, eldest son) drew up some years ago was an excellent source of reference.

Thank you to my agent, Diane Banks, who took an interest in my writing; to Robyn Drury for her great support and considerable help in shaping the book; to Andrea Henry at Transworld for her enthusiasm and editorial skill; and to Becky White for her remarkable attention to detail.

A big thank you to my wife, who helped me with just about everything. And to Pierce and Annie for giving birth to six girls.

A Note on the Author

Kath pictured with her son, J. M. (James) Maloney, in the garden at Lynton Road.

J. M. MALONEY is a former national newspaper showbiz editor and has worked in senior roles in consumer magazines. He is now a freelance showbusiness journalist, who writes for various publications in the UK, Australia and New Zealand. He has written books on the Duke and Duchess of Cambridge, as well as a review examining the stories behind 100 historic newspaper headlines.

As the son of one of the Jarman sisters, he is perfectly placed to tell the story of the experiences of his mother and aunts during the Second World War.

Jim Maloney can be contacted via Twitter @JM_Maloney.